JEAN
ALESI

Other books by the same author:

AYRTON SENNA
His full car racing record

NIGEL MANSELL
The Lion at Bay

MICHAEL SCHUMACHER
Defending the Crown

GERHARD BERGER
The Human Face of Formula 1

AYRTON SENNA
The Legend Grows

JAMES HUNT
Portrait of a Champion

GRAND PRIX SHOWDOWN!
The full drama of the races which decided
the World Championship 1950–92

TWO WHEEL SHOWDOWN!
The full drama of the races which decided
the World 500cc Motor Cycle Championship
from 1949

TORVILL AND DEAN
The full story

As part of our ongoing market research, we are always pleased to receive comments about our books, suggestions for new titles, or requests for catalogues. Please write to: The Editorial Director, Patrick Stephens Limited, Sparkford, Nr Yeovil, Somerset BA22 7JJ.

JEAN ALESI

BEATING THE ODDS

Christopher Hilton

PSL
Patrick Stephens Limited

First published in 1996

British Library Cataloguing-in-Publication Data:
A catalogue record for this book is
available from the British Library

ISBN: 1 85260 547 2

Library of Congress catalog card no. 95 79123

Patrick Stephens Limited is an imprint of Haynes Publishing,
Sparkford, Nr Yeovil, Somerset BA22 7JJ.

Designed and typeset by G&M, Raunds, Northamptonshire
Printed in Britain by Butler & Tanner Ltd, London and Frome

Contents

Acknowledgements

THANKS TO Jose Alesi for particular kindnesses, Thierry Lecourt, Eric Bernard, Eddie Jordan, Harvey Postlethwaite, Ken Tyrrell, John Thompson, Martin Donnelly, Fabien Giroix, Trevor Foster; Cecile Astenave of Renault; Simon Taylor, Managing Director of Haymarket Magazines Limited for kind permission to quote from *Autosport*; Simon Arron, Editor, *Motoring News* for kind permission to quote from that; the bookshop Chater and Scott for supplying back numbers of magazines; Simon de Lautour of the Winfield Driving School; Steve Nichols of McLaren International, formerly of Ferrari; Monica Meroni of Scuderia Italia. I have found *Special Jean Alesi* by *Speciale Formule 1* (Boulogne) extremely useful.

Straight from the grid

GLIMPSES OF THE real thing: first qualifying, Spa, August 1995 and a lone blood-red Ferrari came from the murk, its tyres digging cascades of spray from the sodden track. As it reached towards La Source hairpin it shivered across standing water making little jerks, left–right–left. The driver curved the car outwards to circle La Source. It circled.

Gloved hands soothed and smoothed the steering wheel, constantly adjusting the balance between maintaining speed and losing control. The Ferrari's impetus carried it, nearly floating, towards the metal barrier at the far side of the hairpin. The gloved hands steadied it, turned it towards the downhill rush past the old pits.

The Ferrari suddenly broke left but the driver caught that. It broke right so violently that it was momentarily enveloped in the spray, a shroud of it. The Ferrari headed for a concrete wall a few metres away and two men behind the wall instinctively ducked. The driver caught the Ferrari before the wall and set off at immense speed. A television commentator, John Watson, was murmuring "Jean Alesi has to be very careful. He will not get away with showing contempt to this circuit . . ."

Two weeks before, Alesi had signed for another team, Benetton, for 1996. It was a completely new beginning and perhaps a real chance at the World Championship. Two months before, and after seven years of trying, Alesi had won his first Grand Prix in Canada. He had nothing to prove that August day at Spa, which makes what he did all the more endearing and profound. He knew no other way to drive the car.

It is the core of this book.

A former team-mate captures Alesi's approach in two crisp, almost crackling words: *full attack*.

From 1983, when he began in the turbulent world of Renault 5 turbos, to Australia and his final race for Ferrari in 1995, this French son of a Sicilian immigrant was entirely consistent. He raced as a born racer would. That carried implications, of course, not least that the *heat* of his Latin genes sometimes boiled within the *heat* of the races. His years are strewn with explosions and implosions, hard words and generous acts, tears of anger and tears of delight. When he took the lead in Canada and could envisage the first win, he cried so hard within the cockpit that, every time he braked, the tears covered his visor and he couldn't see where he was going. He had a severe talk with himself about that and made no mistake to the finishing line.

Across the years of waiting — a saga and a torment, as we shall see — he was the most exciting driver in Grand Prix racing: not the most effective or the most economical but somehow raw as racers are and, maybe, should be. Often enough, watching the Ferrari being hurled at places like La Source, you'd find yourself thinking *this is it, this is really what racing is about*.

Steve Nichols, car designer at Ferrari when Alesi arrived there in 1991, ruminates on the theme. "Alesi is so emotional, so enthusiastic, he pushes so much because he's got the natural ability and talent to do it. He cannot, I think, logically accept the limitations of the car when it's slower than some of the others. He attempts to push beyond its limits to *make* it go as fast. He's a little over the limit a lot of the time. In qualifying you can see he's wringing its neck and he won't give up.

Right *A new world: Jean Alesi prepares to test the Benetton in Portugal, late 1995 – and wears plain overalls because he's still contracted to Ferrari* (Formula One Pictures).

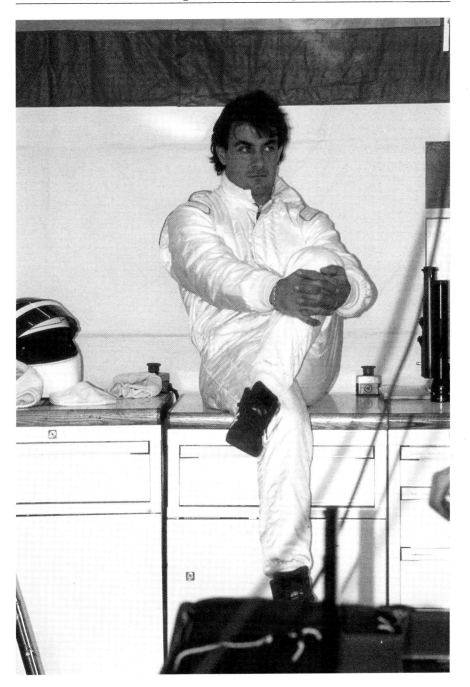

"He's obviously very brave and in the wet he gets spectacular. In some ways, he's a bit of a mixture. Almost contradictory. Some of the races are superb and some of the races he seems to throw it off and spin it off. I tend to think he is *so* competitive and he wants *so* much to go faster that he is not prepared to stop at the limits of the car and you get what you get — including the spectacular."

We might cite examples of undiluted Alesi. Deep into 1995, at the Portuguese Grand Prix, Jean Todt, running Ferrari, ordered Alesi to let team-mate Gerhard Berger through. Alesi refused and exploded on Italian television: "Todt has been a problem for me all year and he has broken my balls. If it has to be like this, I would rather not bother." Ferrari fined him $200,000 and he told Berger it was *good value for money*. I warm to people like that.

Now consider Alesi's last race for Ferrari, the Australian Grand Prix in November. World Champion Michael Schumacher (fearsomely strong and the driver Alesi was replacing at Benetton) went to overtake. Alesi wasn't having any of that and they collided. Because the Championship had been decided two races before, Adelaide lacked overall significance and Alesi could have been forgiven for giving Schumacher a wide berth. Alesi would have violated himself if he had done.

Quite by chance I bumped into him at the Tyrrell factory circa 1990 and in a sense we were both off guard. We just chatted. An impression has always remained with me of that: a chirpy chappie (cheeky, too) with a ready smile and a choirboy face, a bloke thoroughly enjoying being alive.

Nichols judges that "the condition Ferrari has been in these last few years, compared to the English teams, is relative chaos. It makes it more difficult for a driver to thrive. Alain Prost thrived there for a year, 1990. He's cool and calm and methodical, works well with the engineers. Alesi is more Latin, more highly-strung, more emotional and in that type of team it may not be the best of elements. But winning at Ferrari is wonderful because *they* are so emotional and the supporters — the man on the street — they are emotionally involved too." Add Alesi and his own emotion and you had a thunderclap of a thing.

Mind you, that held true all the way through from childhood to here — and will no doubt tomorrow.

• CHAPTER ONE •

In the blood

FRANCO ALESI IS a small, neat, quiet man who speaks softly and has natural charm. This is not everyone's idea of a Sicilian. He came from Alcamo, a seaside town of some 43,000 inhabitants in the north of Sicily. Alcamo lives off fishing, light industry and making typical local wine described as "dry, fresh, fruity, fragrant, with a pale straw-yellow colour." Alcamo is also a holiday resort but more popular with visitors from Palermo, the capital, than foreigners.

In the 1950s the region was extremely poor. Someone has naughtily suggested that Sicilians faced a traditional choice, starve to death or join the mafia. In fact Franco became an apprentice coachbuilder and developed into an artist with a hammer as he shaped metal; yet the future was elsewhere. In 1959 he and two friends decided to look for work in France. One of the friends had a cousin at Carpentras, a town 30 km from Avignon. They'd start there. Franco arrived with a suitcase containing some clothes and his hammer.

He found a job with a local coachbuilder, but at nights took on private metal work to finance his passion — driving in rallies. Between 1961 and 1975 he competed in a whole array of cars, Mini-Coopers, NSUs, Renault-Alpines, Gordinis and finally a Chevrolet Camaro, big and meaty. In time, too, Franco started his own business in Avignon and it prospered.

He married a French girl called Marcelle and they had a family: on 23 September 1962 a son, Guiseppe; on 11 June 1964 a second son, Gianni; on 11 May 1968 a daughter, Cathy. They would not experience the sort of prejudice some immigrants face although, maybe prudently, the boys simply translated their names to the French equivalent. Guiseppe says "I became Joseph (nicknamed Jose) when I entered school, Gianni became Jean. No, we never had any problems with our origins because we lived in the south of France where you find a lot of immigrants. At that time they came from Italy, Spain and Portugal. In fact when Jean and I were little there were many sons of immigrants like us."

Jean spent childhood summers back in Alcamo. "I consider myself French. I grew up within a French culture, and France made it possible for my family to work and raise our living standards but my roots are Italian. I have the character of a Sicilian and my dearest friends seem to be at Alcamo. I was born in France but I was brought up Italian, the food, the thinking."

I'm indebted to Monica Meroni, who has worked in Formula 1 for many years and is from the north of Italy, for a little objective geographical guidance. "Sicilians are typical men of the south. Very strong people, very polite and also very closed, but if you become friends with them they take you to their hearts. They are famous for being passionate, not just in love but in everything. They have a strong passion which holds families together: there is still a *big* feeling about the family. The Sicilians have the blood of the south. They consider Sicily as an island apart from the continent of Europe! They speak with a dialect. When Alesi speaks, he is fluent in Italian but he doesn't always use the words that an Italian might use. I cannot recognise a Sicilian accent. It's strange because I don't know if he speaks in Italian with a French accent or if he speaks more in the Sicilian dialect with a French accent. It's a strange Italian."

The family sensed that Jean preferred playing in the street with his chums on mopeds to studying at school (Jose describes Jean as "a turbulent child but very sincere"). However Franco insisted he complete his secondary education, up to 16, which he did. Then Franco solemnly asked him what he intended to do with his life. Jean replied that he'd like to join the business and "be a racing driver." A familiar adolescent tale and always difficult to quantify: does the

The Eternal Wait is over. The podium, Canada, 11 June 1995 (Formula One Pictures).

teenager foresee his own destiny or just want a hobby which is exciting?

Karting provides a chance to answer both questions. Karts are affordable and reasonably basic and virtually anybody can play. The three dominant drivers in Formula 1 between 1985 and 1993 — Ayrton Senna, Alain Prost and Nigel Mansell — all began like this, buzzing round tight little tracks.

With his background as an active competitor Franco could scarcely refuse Jean the chance. Reflecting, Alesi says: "If I do more 'acrobatics' in a car than other drivers, it is by instinct. I think that every driver must beat himself if he is to win, that there is never a lost cause and it is this desire for victory which pushes you to juggle with the limits. My father, when he competed in rallies, had that spirit and he transmitted it to me."

Certain drivers are born with gifts — Jean is one of them

Franco agreed to buy Jean a kart but with two conditions. The first was that he join the business as a panel-beater, which he did and was shown no favouritism, sweeping the floor like anybody else. The second? "My father was adamant that I had to do everything myself, transport the kart, fix it and so on. I learned a lot about looking after myself." It was 1981. He joined a club at Carpentras, the nearest place where he could race.

In every country the motor racing community — and it is a community — is small compared to mass sports like football. This brings a consequence. Careers interlock and overlap, often from the earliest days; along the way some drivers come and go but others remain as a kind of constant, rising step by step together. What happened with Alesi at Carpentras illustrates this nicely. There he met another teenager, Eric Bernard, and they'd compete in many of the steps, successively Formula Renault, Formula 3, and Formula 3000, and would make their Grand Prix debuts on the same day eight years hence.

The motor racing community is also a mixture of proximity and distance, shared experience and selfish desire, obvious and inherent tension. From the start they all want to win, which means beating each other. Bernard and Alesi became genuine friends but as they advanced the tension deepened and the friendship altered. It is a theme of this book and an important one: even a chummy, cheekie chappie like Alesi could not avoid it.

Bernard says: "In fact we did not race against each other in karting because I ran in the international class and he was in a different category. He was very kind by nature. We became friends and have remained friends though we see each other less often these days. We were together all the time because the same man prepared both our karts. Sometimes I travelled with Jean to act as his mechanic, at the French Championships for instance. I was able to help him. In karting he was very, very quick — just like he is in racing cars — and agile. I remember from time to time lending him my kart — I was in a category superior to his, don't forget — and he was almost as quick as me. That was a point of reference. Certain drivers are born with gifts. I think Jean is one of them."

There's another point about karting. A kart has such adhesion that it can constrict the driver but if he is born with gifts, or nurtures whatever he has, he can express himself within the constriction, particularly in overtaking, cornering and how long his mind tells his body he can wait before braking. He who brakes last seizes the corner (and kart circuits are virtually *all* corners), but if the driver does not have the mental–physical balance he can't do this because Mother Nature will instruct him to brake early for self-preservation. Same in Formula 1.

Alesi won a couple of regional French championships, had a go at moto-cross (and won a junior league) but one way or another cars were the future. *Speciale Formule 1* reports: "His true happiness was to work in the scrapyard next to the factory. There, with a friend, he did up wrecks which he drove to death on a circuit which was marked in the grass of a nearby field. This king of the scrapyard adored suggesting to a client who wanted to buy one of these wrecks 'we'll give it a trial so you can see how well it runs.' The innocent victims clambered into the passenger seat and found themselves carried along on a rodeo ride of such intensity they risked passing out!"

As soon as Alesi had his (road) driving licence he moved into the Renault 5 Turbo Cup. This was not, perhaps, an orthodox step in

The explosive power of Alesi. Monaco, 1992 (Allsport/Vandystadt).

terms of a career because Renault 5s were modified road-going cars, complete unto themselves and distinct from single-seaters — which is where the motorsport steps really lie. Deep down Alesi wanted to be a rally driver like his father, savouring the ability to "throw the cars around" although, as we shall see, he had already discussed with Bernard the possibility of exploring single-seaters. "Renault 5 was cheap and you got good prize money and that was enough to pay for the next race. When I started I tried to have a 'parent', someone to guide me. I tried to have a Formula 1 driver but it was impossible. So I asked Maurice [Trintignant, who competed in F1 from 1950 to 1964] because he lives very close to my house, 30 km. He was very helpful."

The Renault 5 Turbo Cup was famed for its scheming, age differences and general mayhem. Most of the drivers in it have faded into the mists now, although at least one, Fabien Giroix, remains active in motorsport and would interlock with Alesi through Formula Renault, Formula 3 and Formula 3000. "I raced against Jean in 1983. In Renault 5 the racing was crazy. There were a lot of older drivers who'd done it for years but there was also a classification for drivers under 23 and in their first year. We fought together all year, Jean and I, for this classification." Renault 5 was certainly an *entrée* to the community. This first year the little Alesi team comprised Jean, Jose and a mechanic.

"The first time I saw Jean was on the Bugatti circuit at Le Mans [the short circuit as distinct from the full 24-hour sportscar circuit]," Giroix says. "We were doing free practice before the first race and one thing I noticed immediately: he was very fast with the braking, you know he braked so late all the time. His family were there to follow him and they followed him all the time. The family were nice. When I had an accident in Formula 3000 in 1988 his parents wrote me a get well soon letter. That's the sort of people they were."

Alesi finished that first Renault 5 race nineteenth (Giroix eighteenth), was disqualified at the race after but then finished sixth — which is where he could really expect to be against the older, wiser men. He did, however, win round nine at Nogaro in early September, beating Jean-Pierre Pla and Jean-Claude Dutrey, and where are they today? He was seventh in the Championship, Giroix fourth. Interestingly, in answer to my question *could YOU tell he was going to be good?* Jose replies "no, it was impossible to know at the beginning."

"What was it like to race against him?" Giroix muses. "Well, he was then as he is now — very Mediterranean! He do always the attack, you know, he was always like this even in Renault 5. It was a very big fight but it was not dangerous, no, no, no, never. It was always correct but hard."

Alesi is candid about this initial year of car racing. "I was quite fast but I did not have the necessary experience. The races were mostly won by drivers between 35 and 40 years old and they were a bit more sly than me. They knew the game. It was a little crazy but fun and I won at Nogaro. I told my brother to have a go at Ledenon [the second last race] and he did one lap and then rolled it! After that he stuck to running the cars."

While the mayhem was going on, Alesi had not forgotten single-seaters. During 1983 he went to the famous Winfield Driving School,

Main picture *The raw combat of Renault 5 in 1983* (Thierry Bovy, DPPI).

Inset *The move up to Formula Renault in 1984* (J-L Taillade, Automedia).

based at the Paul Ricard circuit in Provence, and so did Bernard. The school gave primary lessons to novices in handling single-seaters, but it was more subtle and perhaps pervasive than that. Each year the better pupils graduated to a competition with a shoot-out final. The winner became *Pilote Elf*, meaning he'd be financed by the oil company into the first step, Formula Renault, the following season. For the impoverished young driver (and most are), *Pilote Elf* was much more than a title. It opened up a real, guaranteed chance to fashion the career; but only one driver could win. For the first time the Alesi-Bernard friendship came under stress.

"Because we were both together all the time in karting, we said to each other *one day we'll do Winfield together*," Bernard explains. "We have an age difference, however. Jean is six months older than me. I thought Jean would go to the school a year before I did because you have to have a driving licence and obviously he'd have his six months earlier. Then he decided to go the same year as me. I didn't know he'd be there.

"Jean already had the experience in Renault 5 which I didn't have. I had no experience of racing cars. It was then that we became less of friends because it was a question of winning. It's always difficult, this, and our friendship was not as strong as it had been in karting. I *had* to try and win the final. I was 19, I couldn't go on and on karting, it was important to race cars but I had no money. All my fees for Winfield were paid by the Karting Federation because I'd been French champion several times. It was a chance I couldn't back away from."

What happened at Winfield would be controversial and demonstrate how the most promising driver does not subsequently have the best career. Simon de Lautour, one of the moving forces behind the school, describes it. "Jean and Eric started with us in July 1983. Jean was a paying customer but sometimes — as with Eric, and Alain Prost [*Pilote Elf* 1975] — they come with a scholarship from karting which is paid direct to the school. Eric was a determined little fellow even from his very humble background and, in fact, he'd been here spectating as a kid and watched Prost's final. Eric told me that later.

"What impression did Jean make? A bit like Prost, like all these guys who are talented: they do the job. If they are smart they don't try and go over the top, they don't do any more than is asked of them. All you need is put them amongst good drivers. His father was always very present. It was your typical Sicilian family, very, very close. Jean was racing in the Renault 5 Cup but I tend to think it gives them more of a psychological advantage than a real one. The Renault 5 was *so* different to racing single-seaters. In the former they pushed, they shoved, they exchanged paintwork and so on, which you don't do in single-seaters for obvious reasons.

"The cars we used were Martini Formula Renaults, which is what they are going into the following year. They had 125-odd horsepower, wings, normally aspirated engines and weighed about 450 kilos. We made them slightly tamer than the competition cars, slightly softer sprung and the ride a little bit higher off the ground so there was some suspension movement and some feed-back given to the pupil." (To interpret this, the cars were reasonably sophisticated — adjusting wings allowed the aerodynamics of the car to be refined — and suspension movement allowed the driver to feel what the car was doing and maybe calculate why it was doing it.)

Bernard was the man to beat — Alesi was a 'tryer' who developed

---

"The format was similar to now. It began with a three-day basic course which took them through to a certain level and then they came back for another session of fast lapping in preparation for the selections to the semi-finals and *Pilote Elf* final. The selections always take place in October. This is where your better pupils are competing against each other. Up to then we put a lot more emphasis on their driving than their times. At the selections it gets harder with the naked eye to differentiate between the excellent and the just good, so times become a lot more important. At that stage from, say, the top 10 you will find your five finalists for the *Pilote Elf*. By the selections we have a pretty high standard and 1983 was a good year. Jean was among the quickest.

"The interesting thing to point out is that never, in our minds, was Eric ever really threatened. Throughout his scholastic year with us he was the man to beat. Jean might well have felt all along that Eric was beatable, but seen from the outside — from the side of the track — it looked like Eric had it buttoned up; as much as you can, anyway, because [at this stage of a career] you never have. Certainly Eric was the dominant factor." Jean, he says, was "a tryer" who developed.

"After our semi-finals, which normally consist of 10 to 12 pupils, we select the best five and train them up, do a teaching programme at the school's expense because our idea is to put on a decent show at the final. We give them two or three days of just driving the car that we have prepared for the final. We finish our training with a mock final and there is some importance to this because the guy who puts in the best performance can choose his start position in the final." Inescapably this is a mental examination of the driver. Should he be confident enough to lead the way and intimidate the others with a fast time — but by doing that offer them a target — or be canny and lie in wait? Bernard elected to go after Alesi . . .

"Eric was quickest in the mock final and confirmed what I had felt all along, that he was the man to beat. The final, on 5 November, was a total of 10 laps: four to warm up, five which were timed, and a cool-off lap. There is an independent *Elf* jury which lays down the rules and we at the school are at the jury's disposal, nothing more. We do whatever the jury asks us to do. Ken Tyrrell was President of the jury for many years [but not 1983]. He once said there are not many events in a driver's life which are quite so intense as trying to win a school final because there is so little room for error in the timed laps and the result is so important to the driver. Remember you're dealing mostly with kids who have only done karting or, in Jean's case, some Renault 5." It's the big chance.

"Jean put up a good performance. Eric went out and of his five laps four were incredibly quick but he spun on the other one. He made that mistake at the chicane. We were on the short circuit and the chicane is not like a lot of those artificial ones you get on modern Grand Prix circuits which are entirely designed to slow the cars. It's a very fast right-hander followed by a tighter left-hander, and losing control there is not difficult, particularly when you're really trying. I'd describe it as the most *selective* part of the circuit.

"I felt *oh well, it's a shame Eric has spun himself out of the competition.* Clearly Jean's average over his five laps was going to be better than Eric's because the spin was costing Eric too much time. After the drivers had done their runs the jury convened and discussed what they should do about it. They decided that Eric's very fast laps justi-

A man between two worlds. Comfortable in Sicily (Formula One Pictures).

fied him having a run-off with Jean. I suppose in many ways they were right because, as they said, the idea is to try and find which driver has the most potential or the greater chance of becoming the driver Elf should back. If they had stuck strictly to the rules Eric would have been out. I must say I thought the jury was being very good to Eric because in my mind he'd blown it — much to my chagrin, really, but just one of those things. Anyway the jury said that if Eric was to have another chance Jean must have another chance, too.

"When they went out again it didn't slow Eric. He went for it as a man with absolutely nothing to lose, but what surprised me more was that Jean didn't pull out all the stops. He was in a position of not having much to lose either, but basically he didn't put up the fight that Eric put up — quite unlike Jean because the man we have come to know in later years is just not like that at all. Watching Jean in qualifying at Grands Prix these days he is just not the same animal.

"Eric won and Jean was clearly disappointed. His father reacted verbally as the President of the jury made the announcement, some comment like *having an Italian name doesn't help* — which was ridiculous, just a spark of emotion. The man was bitterly disappointed and it was an understandable reaction. Jean, I think, was just very, very disappointed. [One report suggests it was an uncle who reacted verbally and a member of the jury told him "Bernard for Ligier, Alesi for Ferrari" — meaning the 'real' Frenchman for a French team in the future, the 'Italian'-Frenchman for an Italian team. It may be that Jean Alesi still resents these words.]

Jean's main characteristic was and is, that he is brave

"I've had the feeling that Jean thought the school may have had a hand in it. Many people associate the jury's decisions with us but, rightly or wrongly, we are no part of the jury. When the jury have decided, they tend to ask me to join them in the office and give me the result before they announce it publicly. They ask *how does that compare with your findings before the final?* and I'll either reply *well, that's a bit of a surprise* or more normally *well, it confirms what we have seen all along*. But this is distinctly afterwards. I think Jean did feel that I had a hand in this. Ronald Reiss [Winfield instructor who had been teaching Alesi] however told him that I felt with the rules the way they were he should have won."

Bernard remembers "I had this second chance and I was quicker still. The jury also gave Jean a second chance and he wasn't as quick. I became *Pilote Elf*. The circumstances were normal for a final: the jury is the sole judge, but our friendship crumbled a bit further. He was desolated. The rivalry between us was extremely strong at that time but, being perfectly honest, the result of the final was good. By that I mean Jean had parents with money to help him into Formula Renault and truly I had no money. My parents were workers. For that reason it was crucial for me to get into Formula Renault the way I did. In the end all was well: Jean knew he was quick and had parents to help, I knew I was quick but I didn't have the parents to help and we were both able to progress." The interlocking and overlapping? A driver called Bertrand Gachot was among the five finalists. He made his Grand Prix debut on the same day as Alesi and Bernard.

In 1984 Bernard moved up to Formula Renault as of right, and Alesi and Giroix moved up there too. The cars were Martinis but turbo-charged. Alesi didn't enjoy this much "because of the turbos. Some teams had special engines and some were playing around with the boost and it was difficult to know where you stood." This year the little Alesi team comprised Jean, Jose and two mechanics. They travelled to the races by car, towing the racing car on a trailer.

Giroix says that "when we started Formula Renault, Jean had his own team and he suffered problems finding a good set-up for the car. In fact he had so many problems he finished a long way down in the championship. He was disappointed. I remember one time at Croix-en-Ternois [the eighth race of the series] he didn't know any more where he was with the car, he didn't understand the car, and it was extremely difficult for him. There were good teams in the formula and good drivers — Yannick Dalmas, Michel Trolle, Bernard and so on.

"The point was that not only did Jean have these problems setting the car up but the other teams had a lot of experience: not just to set-up their cars but knowing which set-up for which circuit. Jean was doing it himself with his brother. Jean went to all his friends — because at this time the drivers were all friends — and asked about the set-ups . . ."

A journalist, Thierry Lecourt, covered these races and offers another insight. "Jean's main characteristic was, and is, that he is brave. When he started in Formula Renault he had very, very bad results because there was a lot of difference between the turbo engines."

In the championship Bernard came seventh and Alesi tenth.

He stayed in Formula Renault in 1985 and was clearly better, with a second place at Le Mans as his best result. But Bernard took the championship, Alesi was fifth, and the friendship got strained further. Bernard recalls: "I had a very good year with an old car — the car from the year before — because I still had no money, although Elf helped with a little budget. Despite the fact that I won, Jean was always an adversary because he was so quick."

The straining? De Lautour explains that "we — Winfield —

Comfortable in Avignon
(Allsport/Vandystadt).

helped Eric in that in 1985 I lent him the car and he was run by Gerard Camilli (Winfield man and team manager). Our team was started with Eric, and Jean was not based in it — he was more of a privateer with his own structure — but Gerard was very present in giving him advice and help. I don't know whether this didn't create a little animosity in the sense of Eric asking *why are you helping Jean?* although I never had the impression that it did.

"As far as I was concerned, Jean was a former Winfield pupil and a finalist and if ever we can help any of our finalists, well, it's almost like an after-sales service. However, I would have thought by the nature of today's sport, by the pressure put on the drivers both commercially and in a sporting manner, that it's too much to be able to nurse those sort of friendships."

Here three witnesses describe 1985. The first is Eric Bernard. "That year we had Gerard Camilli who prepared our cars and we both had the same material. It's true it was tense. In Formula 3 it was more tense. We were truly fighting and it was important for our respective careers so the tension increased." The journalist Thierry Lecourt says: "Jean started to work with Camilli and his results got better. I think his second year in Formula Renault was not, in fact, too bad but he never won a race in the formula." Alesi himself recalls: "I felt I was wasting my parents' money so I decided to quit. It was my father who stopped me from doing that. He said we had to be sure that it was not the car which was holding me back. So the year after that we bought a Formula 3 car" — and prepared for the tension with Bernard to increase.

• CHAPTER TWO •

Stormy weather

FORMULA 3 IS arguably the moment when the career takes its true shape. By now there are signs about the driver, incidents, glimpses which with hindsight assume more than temporal importance. To cover this, I propose to quote contemporary race reports (composed without time for reflection) and for them I'm grateful to *Autosport* and Thierry Lecourt.

"Jean went into Formula 3 directly, with his own team, in 1986," Lecourt says. "It was the same team that he had in Formula Renault, brother Jose, his father, his mother, two mechanics. He had a little truck. Because the family came from Italy they knew a lot of people at Dallara [an Italian manufacturer] and Jean was the first person to race a Dallara in France.

"The car was very, very good and with the standard set-up Jean was able to go well. They were clever when they chose the car and clever when they chose the engine, Alfa Romeo, because virtually everybody else was using Volkswagen engines. At the beginning it seemed a gamble. In fact, as it turned out, it wasn't. I remember the first race in 1986, Nogaro. He qualified third and finished second behind Dalmas [of the mighty ORECA team, of which more later]."

In his report Lecourt wrote: *At the start, with a faint drizzle around, it was Alesi, on his debut, who got the drop on the field with Fabien Giroix in his wake and the ORECA twins Dalmas and Trolle snapping at his heels. A surprised Alesi led for 14 laps. Eventually Dalmas closed on Alesi, setting fastest lap and, experience coming to the fore, took the lead.*

Alesi finished almost 30 seconds behind. "I could have won but I weakened mentally at the end."

The glimpses of Nogaro are important. Giroix says: "Jean came with the Dallara. I was with Dave Price [a Brit running a team in French Formula 3] and we had a Reynard and the Reynard was really good at the beginning of the race but the tyres went off. Before that we do a very big fight, Dalmas, Trolle, Jean and me. For Jean that proved something because Trolle had long experience of Formula 3, Dalmas too, and I had had the year before in it. And Jean came in with his Dallara and he was quick immediately. Had he changed as a man since I'd known him in Formula Renault two years before? He never changed. He was like he is today, always really friendly. Now if you see him at a Grand Prix he comes over very soon to speak to you. He hasn't a big head or anything like that."

Alesi finished fifth at Albi, qualified 0.31 seconds behind Dalmas and finished second to Trolle at Magny-Cours. There's a temptation to read too much into this, however much he'd visibly improved. Lecourt puts it in context. "It was not extraordinary for a little team to do well because in France there was only one big team, ORECA, and the situation in Formula 3 was a very particular one. All the French drivers tried to use Martini cars because Martini was French, and it was always like that — ORECA won the championship with a Martini.

"Formula 3 was just starting back from nowhere in France and we had no experience with cars like Reynard or Ralt — or Dallara! The Martini in 1986 was not such a good car. Jean made a lot of jokes, he was happy to be there. It was, I think, a dream for him to be a racing driver. He was very friendly and he was close to Philippe Gache [another driver] who was also beginning in Formula 3 with his own team. They were always together joking in the paddock. Jean was also very concentrated on the racing. He knew what he wanted and that was to win the races. He was working hard for that.

"It's easier to finish well in Formula 3 than in some other categories because the cars are not powerful. You've seen a lot of drivers winning in Formula 3 and never winning a race after — they might

The old friend and foe, Eric Bernard, giving Frank Williams a ride in a Renault Espace. Alesi might have signed to drive for Williams in 1991 (ICN UK Bureau).

even be *bad* in Formula 3000 or Formula 1 — because if you have a good Formula 3 car with a good set-up you can be quick. Of course that was not the case with Jean because he was quick when he reached Formula 3000 and quick when he reached Formula 1, but I don't think Formula 3 is the place where you prove if you have talent or not."

Alesi took his Dallara to Monaco for the annual and important support race to the Grand Prix. The Formula 1 moguls might be watching and might not forget what they saw. That apart, it was an opportunity to measure yourself against international competition, moving out of your domestic community to the larger one. Drivers from 11 countries competed. Ten of them would reach Formula 1. Among these was a quiet Ulsterman called Martin Donnelly, then in British Formula 3. "I hadn't paid much attention to Jean's career at the time. I remember the transporter he had — well, just a small, poxy van with one racing car beside it out at the front of the paddock. I thought *that looks pretty basic.* If you don't see a big, flashy outfit you think they won't do much — but on the track he was up there. That was my first impression of Jean."

He qualified thirteenth of 32: only the fastest 22 made the race. *Autosport* reported:

Fifth was the subject of a keen scrap between [Harald] Huysman, [Eugenio] Visco and Alesi. The trio became a duo when Visco lost it at the chicane. Alesi made a bid for the inside line of the Loews hairpin and contact was made when Harald tried to shut the door. Alesi emerged from the chicane ahead but with a deflating tyre and showed his frustration by weaving all the way to Tabac, where he ran wide and ceded the place to Huysman again.

Alesi retired after 17 of the 24 laps. He returned to French Formula 3 and at Pau, as Jose says, "he was second after the opening lap but the transmission broke and he had to stop"; at La Chatre he came third. At Rouen, Lecourt wrote:

Frederic Delavallade did not have it easy because the race was led most of the way by poleman Jean Alesi, once again showing fine form in his Dallara. The two indulged in some wheel-banging and protests were flying by the end of the day. They crossed the line just 0.07 apart although later Alesi was excluded for dangerous driving.

After the usual mid-season break (the whole of France goes on holiday in August) the season resumed at Albi in September. Lecourt wrote:

The F3 men were back in action and Jean Alesi put his name in the record books. He gave Dallara its first win in the French Formula 3 championship as he romped to victory in glorious conditions. The Avignon driver was safely on pole aided by the fact that championship leader Yannick Dalmas was suffering from a badly sprained wrist. Alesi's task was helped greatly by a collision involving his three closest challengers on the grid, Michel Trolle, Gilles Lempereur and Paul Belmondo. In a hefty accident all three were out and Trolle was taken to hospital. Alesi emerged at the end of the first lap with a lead of some six seconds over Eric Bernard, who had started sixth on the grid. Bernard held second place for five laps, fighting off the challenge of Delavallade, Lempereur and Dalmas, but inevitably these more experienced drivers came through. The race however belonged to Jean Alesi.

He beat Delavallade by more than nine seconds. A week later at Le Mans:

Jean Alesi scored his second successive victory at a canter. Alesi qualified on pole and led away from the start chased by Dalmas and Trolle in the

ORECA Martinis. On the third lap Trolle and Dalmas tangled.

Alesi beat Trolle by more than two seconds to make the championship Dalmas 110, Delavallade 73, Alesi 71, and two rounds to go. At Ledenon:

In third place was recent pace-setter Jean Alesi once he had removed the challenge of the promising Bernard — knocking him off the track. The action in this area was fraught indeed, with Philippe Gache and Eric Bachelart also coming to blows.

It rained hard during the final race at Croix-en-Ternois. Trolle led. Alesi, Dalmas, Bachelart and Gache squabbled, Bachelart forced his way up to second but spun on the fourth lap and Alesi inherited the position. Dalmas, on a charge, thrust by to give a race result of Trolle, Dalmas, Alesi, and a championship of Dalmas 118, Alesi 78, Trolle 76.

It was tight, with 17 cars within a second of Alesi's pole time

---

"In 1986 and 1987," Lecourt says, "the French Formula 3 championship was the best it has ever been. For example in 1987 you had Jean, Eric Bernard, Erik Comas, Fabien Giroix, Paul Belmondo, Cathy Muller, Philippe Gache, Eric Bachelart — the Belgian guy who is now driving IndyCars. The level was becoming higher, more good teams, more difficult to win. Jean's problem was that when he finished second in 1986 he knew he was capable of winning the championship but he knew he had to go to ORECA because it was possible for him to have Marlboro backing there — very important — and, for sure, to be in the number one team, the best team, favourites for the championship."

In 1987 Alesi joined ORECA who, under their team principal Hughes de Chaunac, had a long pedigree, helping such as Prost, Rene Arnoux and Thierry Boutsen on their steps to Formula 1.

"The problem," Lecourt says, "was that ORECA chose Martini cars and the car was really a disaster. Jean pushed very hard to go back to Dallara. The first race was at Albi and he was far from the pace. All the Dallaras were in front, and the Ralts." Lecourt wrote:

The biggest surprise of all was the poor performance of the ORECA

Left First steps into French Formula 3, 1986 (Olivier Marguerat, DPPI).

team Martinis which have dominated the championship for the last four seasons. Team leader Jean Alesi could only qualify 21st with his team-mate Jacques Goudchaux 23rd. In the race the two stormed up through the field but by the end were still only 12th and 14th.

Giroix won. "I had the same car as Jean [a Dallara — Alesi would abandon the Martini and return to Dallara, as we shall see], the same engine and he has Italian blood in him, you know. To the guy who made the engines Jean was like his second son. This year he made very good engines. Jean and I, we had a big 'fight.' It was not an *angry* fight but for me Jean was the driver to beat and for Jean I was the driver to beat. It was exciting with the two teams — he with ORECA, me with Saulnier — and we didn't have such good personal contact during the year because there was so much pressure during it to beat the other." The strain on friendship again, not to mention the strain between Alesi and de Chaunac over which car to use.

Lecourt observed as Alesi "pushed de Chaunac to change the car. For the second race, at Nogaro, he did convince de Chaunac to use his own Dallara from 1986! He took pole and won the race." It was tight, 17 cars within a second of Alesi's pole time.

For this one meeting Alesi had switched from his ORECA Martini MK52 to his old Dallara 386. The car was run by ORECA for the weekend and Alesi was flying. From pole he led away under intense pressure from Bernard. The two diced throughout the event but despite setting fastest lap Bernard could not overtake Alesi.

"They pushed Tico Martini to make a lot of modifications to make the car more competitive and in the third race, Magny-Cours, Jean had the Martini again," Lecourt says. "Although it was better than it had been at Albi, this proved to be the last race with Martini."

At Magny-Cours Alesi qualified ninth and finished seventh (championship: Gache 35, Bernard 32, Alesi fifth on 18). "They bought a new Dallara under pressure from Marlboro because for de Chaunac it was very important to win the championship. ORECA always won the championship! It was completely forbidden *not* to win the championship! They had the best budget — double anybody else's — the best team, the best car, the best drivers, it was the best package so they were *obliged* to win! "De Chaunac had to be clever, he knew he had to make the right choice and after Magny-Cours they changed to Dallara. Jean was far adrift in the championship, which Bernard was leading. Jean had to fight very hard to catch Bernard, race by race, little points by little points. It was an extremely difficult championship."

At Dijon, with Alesi in a fourth different car for the fourth race, Bernard took pole from him by 0.04 of a second. The Dallara 387 was brand new and virtually 'unsorted' which made Alesi's performance more remarkable. He led for eight laps until Bernard overtook him and it stayed like that (championship Bernard 48, Gache 43, Alesi 31). Then he won at Ricard.

In the Monaco Grand Prix support race Alesi qualified second behind Frenchman Didier Artzet and spent the race "stalking" him. He couldn't catch him any more than a certain Johnny Herbert could catch Alesi.

Artzet	39m 32.423s
Alesi	39m 33.455s
Herbert	39m 46.063s

At Pau in French Formula 3, Lecourt says that "the race was scheduled for 6pm on the Sunday after 3000 practice. Very suddenly a storm started — well, it wasn't a storm, it was a tornado. All the trees in the paddock fell." *Autosport* reported:

A formidable wind devastated the central paddock area leaving 21 people injured beneath fallen trees, awnings and torn-down marquees. The ferocity of the phenomenon was estimated at 65–70 mph. Aged trees, some 80ft high, came crashing down with terrifying results. The cars had been in grid formation as the wind howled in, sounding like a massive helicopter, showering the packed area with tree boughs and splinters.

The race was postponed until the following day. Alesi won and was now deep into a winning sequence. At Rouen, Lecourt wrote:

As the leaders came thundering towards the blind brow down into the sweepers, Gache saw yellow flags and slung on the anchors, unsure what might unfold below. As he did so, Alesi, Giroix, Bachelart, Comas, Delavallade and Bernard all went by like a train leaving him a smarting seventh! Alesi eked out a small lead over the duelling Giroix and Bachelart.

At Paul Ricard, Alesi had pole but 15 cars were covered by just one second.

From lap 20 onwards Bernard was on the Dallara's tail, but the fleet Alesi moved just far enough on the straights to stop Bernard taking the lead. On several occasions the two touched wheels as they fought it out, but when the flag came Alesi was ahead by a car's length.

At La Chatre after the mid-summer break Alesi took pole and led throughout with Bernard and Comas in pursuit (championship Alesi 108 points, Bernard 107, Giroix 64). At Nogaro, Alesi took pole again and won an "exciting" race by 11 seconds. Bernard spun after three laps (Alesi 124, Bernard 108, Giroix 67). At Le Mans:

Alesi could have wrapped it all up but it was not to be, a coming-together with championship rival Bernard on lap 3 eliminating the Avignon driver. Bernard suffered a puncture and failed to add to his points total.

At Ledenon, Bernard took pole and led throughout.

Alesi qualified second but messed up his start (having already crashed in the warm up) and fell behind Didier Artzet, thereafter following the Monaco F3 winner for the duration.

Alesi 135, Bernard 123, Giroix 82. Giroix remembers that at Ledenon "Jean had good lap times, he was good in qualifying and I think he needed to win to take the championship. You know he had something inside him which always made him want to push further.

The French Formula 3 Championship in 1987. Moving to third place at Croix-en-Ternois, the last and decisive race (P. Azemberger, DPPI).

Sometimes he didn't think of the championship, only to be quickest.

"It is the same in Formula 1 now. You see him driving in the rain during qualifying and always he wants to show that he is quick in the rain, and he takes some risks. He does not think 'OK, this afternoon it's not necessary because it's raining.' No, he thinks it is always necessary to be the quickest and to take the risks to be the quickest. At Ledenon I followed him in the warm-up on race morning and he tried so hard he went off and had the crash. It was a small crash but the car suffered a lot of damage."

At Croix-en-Ternois, Alesi needed only be fifth to take the championship even if Bernard won.

Artzet claimed the pole and led in the early stages pressed by Alesi. When Eric Bachelart began to exert heavy pressure Alesi decided to play safe and let him go.

That is at odds with Ledenon's description of Alesi and perhaps mirrors the contradictions within the man. Bernard was fifth. The championship: Alesi 144, Bernard 130, Bachelart 86. "We went into French Formula 3 together," Bernard says, "and truly the first year Jean was better than me, then the next year he won the championship and I was second, although I'd always been in the lead until near the end of the season. It had been a very, very tight struggle. We'd battled the whole time. When I finished first he was second, when he finished first I was second! Jean had a Dallara and I had a Ralt. The Ralt had less top speed and unfortunately I couldn't do more than be runner-up. The rest were a long way behind us.

"Our friendship still existed because we had a profound respect for one another. I believe Jean has always thought I was a quick guy, and I always thought Jean was a quick guy. We'd had the strong friendship in karting and despite competing so hard we'd remained close. But it is clear that as young drivers — when you are battling the whole time for the same objectives — you cannot have the same friendship as before. It is no longer possible. The respect, however, remained. We never did dirty things to each other, we never crashed into each other in Formula Renault or Formula 3 even though we were battling so hard." This does not seem a trick of memory but a way of saying that the "coming together" at Ledenon was not serious enough to be classified as a crash.

Alesi was poised to take the next step, which would place him

Alesi would always be happy driving anything fast. Here he takes a Ferrari to third place in an IMSA race at Laguna Seca, California, in 1989 (Gilles Levent, Automedia).

permanently in the international motor racing community. The next step was called the Marlboro Test. There he'd meet Donnelly — third in the British F3 championship — again. Nineteen drivers from various European competitions were invited to the test, held at Donington in mid-October. The format resembled Winfield. Those on the verge of Formula 3000 were given a 10-lap run in Stefano Modena's championship winning March on the Wednesday and a proper 25-lap run on the Thursday.

"Marlboro were very good at doing things like that," says Donnelly. "It was a big PR test and big recognition for young drivers. You had the 25 laps and one set of new tyres. You could change whatever you liked on the car, springs, gear ratios and so on. You went out on old tyres and it was up to you as and when you wanted to go onto the new tyres. Modena set a pace time."

That was 1m 02.33s. Then Volker Weidler (from Kremer Porsche sportscars) did 1m 03.06s, Italian Formula 3 champion Enrico Bertaggia 1m 03.47s and Alesi, as French Formula 3 champion, 1m 03.00s. Alesi was quickest of them all, exploiting his new tyres to the full. Donnelly, fastest on the Wednesday (which didn't count, of course) couldn't make his full run — darkness fell! He was given a subsequent test, did 1m 01.90s and said "I know I did a good job and over the last eight laps I was really enjoying it. The car felt perfect and I am getting used to the power."

Marlboro would sponsor two Formula 3000 teams in 1988, Onyx based in Sussex, and ORECA. That in turn meant sponsoring four drivers, two in each team. The importance is self-evident. Formula 3000 was *the* decisive step before Formula 1 and if you were in a leading team your chances of getting there improved in direct proportion.

Reflecting, Donnelly says: "The thing that sticks in my mind is that I was quickest overall by about eight-tenths. I said all the right things and I thought it was looking good. Lo and behold, I think Marlboro Germany put more money in and Weidler got the drive" — with Onyx. Alesi got the drive with ORECA.

"It wasn't a good drive to have."

Footnote to 1987. Alesi contested the Macau Formula 3 race in late November, an event as traditional as the Monaco support race and an occasion when young drivers lived hard and raced hard. The Portuguese enclave near Hong Kong seemed to have been created for both those interesting human activities. *Autosport* reported that Alesi, who'd qualified twenty-first, went "unrebuked" at the start.

His "*white Dallara catapulted out of formation, to the right, and was up four rows, thrusting through third gear in all probability, when the lights changed to green. This most blatant flaunting of the starting system had the French champion weaving and jostling, threading in and out of the main body of wheel-spinning cars before Yacht Club curve, and past Mauricio Gugelmin — who'd qualified eighth. After four laps Alesi, up 13 places or so, smacked into Joachim Winkelhock, cannoning the German's Reynard into Gachot, deranging both suspension and bodywork . . .*

Macau was always a bit like that, so it might be a sign and a portent; and it might not.

• CHAPTER THREE •

Fire burning

ALESI STAYED WITH ORECA for 1988, moving into Formula 3000. Marlboro produced a guide to the season and by way of preview said: "Last year Yannick Dalmas finished fifth having won the races at Pau and Jarama. This year the team has reigning French Formula 3 Champion Jean Alesi and the experienced Pierre-Henri Raphanel to drive its March chassis, and both are regarded as potential champions." They'd meet strong opposition, including Roberto Moreno, Olivier Grouillard, Donnelly, Pierluigi Martini, Gachot, Mark Blundell and Herbert, who'd all reach Formula 1.

The season went wrong for ORECA and Alesi. "It's very difficult to explain," he says. "I had a very bad relationship with an engineer in the team and everything was wrong. When you don't have the team with you, you can do nothing. Everything is important — technicians, mechanics, everyone — they are all a big part of the package. 1988 was terrible, terrible, it was a very, very bad year.

"I had the opportunity to stop [I considered retiring]. I felt so bad in my head. I race because I like to race, I don't like to have problems. The March was not an awful car, it just needed development. We asked for changes to the car after the first race [at Jerez, Alesi eleventh, Raphanel fifteenth] but for Vallelunga [second race, Alesi ninth, Raphanel eighteenth] it was the same and so we bought Reynards."

Lecourt expands on that. "Hughes de Chaunac made a mistake when he chose the chassis because they started the season with Marchs — ORECA had used Marchs in 3000 for a lot of years — but it was the year Reynard arrived and that really was the best car of the championship. Johnny Herbert had one and so did a lot of others. Jean was team-mate to Raphanel and they had many problems at the first race because they were far off the pace, same at the second race. For the third race, Pau, they convinced de Chaunac to buy Reynards. This was very important for Jean because he had the full backing of Marlboro, the car was full Marlboro livery and the level of competition in 3000 was higher with more good teams in it than Formula 3. To win races was more difficult."

He seeks perfection and if he doesn't find it that affects him

Alesi says: "One of the problems was that ORECA had one engineer, Gilles Schaefer, working on two cars. Raphanel was the experienced driver whereas I was regarded very much as the debutante. The team, I think, listened to Pierre-Henri most, and as the season went on Gilles and I were in disagreement more and more. Sometimes things were changed on my car without my knowing."

"The 3000 year was a difficult one," de Chaunac concedes. "We did not have the full budget we needed and so we couldn't offer Jean all he wanted. He's a man who is very gifted, a driver who is intelligent, willing, but he's looking for perfection. If he doesn't find it, that affects him, and because it affects him it affects the people working with him. Prost, of course, is a perfectionist. Alesi is the same but in a different way. He did not accept human error. And yet he is a man who is 'seductive' in the sense that he is gifted, natural, he *communicates* his motivation. He doesn't speak with his head but with his heart — no, the word I use, tripes (guts), is even stronger than heart."

At Pau *Autosport* reported that "Alesi, with only 80 km on the clock of his car, was quickest of all in the preliminary session, a driver's only chance to arrive at a basic chassis balance if he is not to be left behind through wasting vital seconds in the twin 30-minute sessions which determine the grid — of only 22 cars at Pau, remember. Alesi looked mightily impressive throughout, neat and precise, the consistency of his speed formidable also. 'As it is, the car is very competitive but I don't fully understand it yet,' explained Jean, who looked set to join Raphanel on the front row until the last minute, when the psyched up Moreno bagged pole with the flyer he knew he could deliver." Grid:

Moreno 1:10.86

Raphanel 1:11.08

Alesi 1:11.26

Martini 1:11.63

At the green light Moreno moved to mid-track positioning himself for the first corner, a right. Raphanel slotted in behind but Alesi travelled hard up the inside, kept his balance and nerve and followed Moreno through the corner — second. Moreno pulled away while Alesi fended off Raphanel. Alesi finished second, Raphanel sixth. It was almost deceptive: what Alesi could wring from himself and a car round a street circuit. You couldn't do that at circuits like Silverstone where he was fifth (Raphanel third) or Monza where he was thirteenth (Raphanel eleventh).

"Jean made some good finishes," Lecourt remembers, "including second place but the problem was in the team. At this time ORECA had an engineer who was completely involved in the set-up of Jean's car. There were a lot of problems between Schaefer and Jean because they didn't have a good feeling together. Jean was very upset and as the season went on he was really not in good mental shape. I could see that, see how upset he was. He was always criticising what was happening in the team and the way the team was working.

"I remember, for example, Monza. I arrived there and I had not been before. Jean took me with him to show me the track, each corner, everything, and he spoke about the team. He was upset because Schaefer would only set the car up with a computer, there was no way to discuss things, and Schaefer was not listening to the driver's feelings about the set-up. It was a human problem for Jean.

"He is exciting to watch now (1995). He was the same then. He has a very strong character. He was capricious in his racing but only for good reasons. These days if there is a problem with his Formula 1

The troubled Formula 3000 season of 1988. Alesi in qualifying at Brands Hatch (Allsport).

Alesi overtakes Johnny Herbert at Silverstone (Thierry Bovy, DPPI).

Eddie Jordan (left), seen here with his driver Eddie Irvine and Jean Todt of Ferrari in 1995 — Alesi and Gerhard Berger are leaving Ferrari, Irvine and Michael Schumacher are joining (ICN UK Bureau).

car he pulls his helmet off and leaves it in the car, pulls his gloves off and throws them down. It was the same then. He was very passionate, very hot. He was always like that."

Alesi finished sixth at Pergusa (Raphanel fifth) and had a first lap accident at Brands Hatch (Raphanel failed to qualify). In the middle of the pack going up to Druids someone punted Alesi and the car skimmed sideways over the grass, struck the tyre wall backwards and he limped back to the pits to retire. At Birmingham he crashed after 16 laps, hitting a barrier and walking briskly away, tousselling his hair and looking downcast (Raphanel retired on the first lap, accident). He finished twentieth at Le Mans (Raphanel sixth).

Alesi decided on drastic action. Or, as he says, "John Thompson from Reynard came to work with me at Zolder and Dijon and immediately it was better. He listened to what I had to say and made some suggestions which turned out to be in the right direction."

The memory of it amuses Thompson. "I went basically because he'd had enough of his engineer. They said they wanted somebody from the factory and I went along to help them out, that was all. I just went for the two weekends. I'd never met Alesi before and I'd never been to a 3000 race before either! I was on Formula 3 all the time then. I showed up at Zolder and introduced myself to him. His English was all right.

"How did he strike me? He was just good, really. I'd travelled down there on the plane with the guys who normally look after 3000 and sort of asked them *well, what do you do and what do these cars respond to?!* and applied that logic really. It was fairly straightforward and we went all right. We qualified sixth at Zolder, which I was gobsmacked about because he was one of those guys who said 'well, the car's not perfect but it's as good as it's going to get and there's only 10 minutes left. I'll go and do a time.' And he could do that. I was really impressed by him. He made a really good start to the race but he got tangled with Belmondo."

They'd been battling for fifth when they touched.

Belmondo: "Alesi was in trouble with gears and missed one, didn't see me alongside and took me off at the hairpin."

Alesi: "Belmondo tried to pass me on the grass, touched my rear wing and gave me a puncture."

Alesi finished ninth. Thompson says Alesi "split one of the rear

45

wheel rims, came into the pits, changed that and went out and just drove round. Then we went to the next race — Dijon — where he qualified only thirteenth but he finished fifth."

Alesi listening to what Thompson had to say? "Well (chuckle) I didn't know what to do. I had a really *basic* understanding of what needed to be done to a Formula 3000 car which I'd gleaned from the guys on the way down," Thompson says. "I think they sent me because they didn't really have anybody else. I suppose that was it! I got a nice impression of him as a bloke, I really enjoyed it and you get to work with these guys and you don't know they're going to be superstars. You could tell he was good, you could definitely *tell*. He had something about him which said OK, *I'd like to have a terrific car but I can do it anyway*."

Alesi concedes that "morale was pretty low by the final race but with the help I got from John I finished fifth and was one lap ahead of Pierre-Henri." The championship: Moreno 43, Grouillard 34, Donnelly (plucked from British F3 in mid-season by Eddie Jordan because Jordan's regular driver, the Swede Thomas Danielsson, had an eye problem) 30, Alesi tenth on 11, Raphanel thirteenth on 8.

Alesi was close to despair. "I talked it over with my brother and my father and they said to me 'you have to try another time with a good team.'" Alesi knew it must be a team in England, however wary he was because stories crossed the Channel suggesting two drivers in the same team didn't always get equal treatment there.

De Chaunac insists, however, that "despite the fact that we still didn't have a full budget and despite what happened in 1988 I remained so impressed by Jean that I considered throwing the whole weight of ORECA behind him — in effect, running just one car to give him what he needed to do well. And I always said to him not to go too quickly," meaning in life as well as in a car.

In late November Alesi competed at Macau with the Dallara, brother Jose running him. He qualified third in his group although he suffered a broken selector rod on the first day. The 'team' worked hard to make the Dallara controllable over Macau's bumps. The race was run in two heats, Alesi finishing second to Eddie Irvine in the first; in the second he beat Irvine from the start but in the usual first-lap mayhem Bertaggia nipped ahead. Alesi held an aggregate nine second lead over him but on lap seven the German Otto Rensing went by. Alesi had a puncture in the right rear tyre and it could be clearly seen. Across the last few laps it deflated completely and on the final lap he was on the wheel's metal rim. It cost him the race on aggregate.

Where would he go from here?

Lecourt says that "Jean was at the Chamonix ice track all winter with Gache. They'd drive standard cars on the ice, like Citroëns. 1988 was a big disaster because Marlboro stopped sponsoring him and Jean did not want to go with ORECA one more time. At Chamonix at the beginning of February Jean told me he wanted to stop track racing and do some rallying with a Renault 5 turbo. Just after that the deal with Eddie Jordan came. It was made very, very late." (Pausing here briefly: the ice racing, at the French ski resort, was a curious event of six races over a weekend and decided on points. The Armco was walls of snow and many good drivers had a go for the fun of it.)

Eddie was always there, helping
— he was like a part of my family

Jordan, gregarious Irishman and former driver, was now running his Formula 3000 team from modest premises at Silverstone circuit. His hiring of Alesi was a typical motor racing situation, governed by chance. "This is something extremely important," Eric Bernard says, "and it is the truth. When Jean went to Jordan he went there because I refused to join them. It's an interesting story of how Jordan came to give Jean the chance and how his career lifted off from there.

"Jordan wanted to sign me. The team had a budget with Q8 [the fuel company] but for 1989 might have Camel as sponsors. I said to Eddie 'I can't sign because of my connection with Elf' — who had always helped me — 'I can't go with Q8.' I gave a gentleman's agreement to Elf saying that I would sign for them for 1989. The next day Eddie rang me at home and said 'OK, you can't refuse to sign for us now because we are with Camel and I've arranged everything.' With Camel, the Elf problem disappeared [because Camel wouldn't object]. I said 'no, I can't because I gave my word to Elf last night.' It was a decision which is the key to my career and to the career of Jean Alesi."

Simon de Lautour of Winfield watched from afar with a knowing eye. "I think Jean made better decisions than Eric as to who to drive for. He went to ORECA in Formula 3 and Eric stayed with us and we were just beginning. After ORECA, Jean got out and about. So many other French drivers lock into French teams and they end up getting buried if they're not careful. That's one of Jean's strengths: he was prepared to get out and about, that and the fact people became attached to him because he is a warm person."

Jordan hired Alesi. "I lived in England to learn English," Alesi says. "When I went to England for the first time it was like being on the moon. I had no friends, I couldn't speak the language. I was very isolated, but Eddie was always there and he helped me. He became like a part of my family, like Jose my brother."

"It goes back," Jordan says, "to the earliest signs I saw. I read all the magazines covering junior racing and karting and all that. I'd seen his name but not very strong. We had, and always did have, a strong involvement as a team in Europe — a small factory in Nogaro when I ran in French Formula 3. I'd seen this young kid called Alesi being run by his brother. Obviously I went round the outside of the track taking drivers' corner times and so on. I enjoy that and you notice different things: whether a driver is quick through the corners, quick along the straight. You also assess the quality of the team that is running the driver, their attitude, their minds. We evaluate each person on many, many aspects.

"I felt a good feeling about him and in 1987 he did very well in the French championships with de Chaunac. When you're with the ORECA team you always win because it's the best engine, the best car — so it's very difficult to evaluate how good these people are. Then Jean did 3000 and we did 3000. He was with ORECA, we had Johnny Herbert and Martin Donnelly and, of course, we won a lot of races. Jean was a Marlboro driver but basically they sacked him or advised him his future was not there."

Trevor Foster, Jordan's team manager and chief engineer, is sure that "Eddie and I were instrumental in resurrecting Jean's career which, to be honest, had taken a dip. During 1988 we started a relationship with Camel and we ran Johnny Herbert. The relationship reached the point where Camel were talking about running two cars in Formula 3000. We took Martin for 1989 and we spoke with Jean.

His relationship with de Chaunac hadn't worked out, the thing with Marlboro had come to an end and he was desperately looking for the chance to rebuild his career."

Eddie Jordan explains that "I had some trouble because nobody had heard of Alesi in this part of the world. I don't say I had a hell of a job convincing Duncan Lee [Director of Promotion for RJ Reynolds, who owned Camel] but, well, I explained my case to him and he felt that I had a good feel for young drivers. He obviously had markets to consider and other drivers were in a stronger position. Successfully I argued my case. I judged that hopefully there should not be and never should be any compromise on performance in terms of drivers or cars or engines or whatever because ultimately they are all part of the make-up which is the result. I felt that strongly.

"OK, I was putting my neck on the line but I felt good about taking Jean even though people thought I was mad. At that time he had been very, very sketchy apart from that one year in French Formula 3 with ORECA. He was very quiet, shy, very much into family, not out night-clubbing or anything like that. He wanted to be

Alesi, vintage 1989 (Allsport).

with a team in Britain, he wanted to get away from France. He was slightly different in that he comes from a very strong Italian background, the French are very nationalistic and I don't know whether they had accepted him properly or not. He was almost like a nomad so it was quite easy for him to come to England even though it must have been difficult with his family and his fiancée."

Jean and Jose arrived. Foster "went to London to meet them. I took them round to EJM — the Eddie Jordan Management Group — whose head office was in London. We had a long meeting there. Jean was very paranoid about Bernard. At the time Bernard was talking to us as well. Jean thought that Bernard was rated higher than he was, if you like. I think Jean had spoken to other 3000 teams and they'd said 'we are talking to Bernard and we'll let you know.'

"He was absolutely paranoid. He was saying *ah, but what if Bernard goes to this team or goes to that team?* I said *look, it's hard enough for you to decide the right move for your career never mind choosing the right move in relation to what he is going to do.* We decided to go with Jean, we did the deal. The thinking behind it was that Eddie had watched Jean in French Formula 3 and we — Eddie and I — agreed that if you have a pedigree winning in the lesser formulae, which Jean had done, you don't suddenly lose it. And he was certainly very hungry."

The main opposition in 1989: Comas and Bernard (DAMS/Lola), Marco Apicella (First/Reynard), Eric van de Poele (Players Racing/Reynard), Andrea Chiesa (Roni/Reynard), Blundell (Middlebridge Group/Reynard), Irvine and Lehto (Pacific/Reynard), Danielsson (Madgwick/Reynard).

"I insisted as part of the package," Jordan says, "that he lived with us for a while in my house, as we have often done with drivers in the past. I must have the drivers close to me. I need to see them in the gym three, four times a week. I want to be in touch with what they are doing. I need to see what they are eating. I need to know I am not getting something which is just being prepared for me: I want to see them in the good times and the bad times and the average times, I want to get into their mind, I want to establish a rapport that is deeper than just a frequent visit to the workshop by somebody I've hired and who becomes only a hired gun. I need to establish a bond."

Foster captures that. "We put him in a loving environment at Jordan."

Early in March the Jordan team went to Vallelunga for testing. "We had the 1988 car," Foster says, "and the idea was to get a bit of mileage with Jean and Martin. We were there for two or three days. The Pacific team were there with Irvine and JJ Lehto and they had their 1989 cars, the Middlebridge outfit was there with Blundell. They'd got their new cars early and they'd been doing quite a bit of testing. If I remember rightly the quickest time was a low one minute 5 seconds. Martin went first, set the car up, balanced it for the day and did a high four, a one minute 4.7 seconds, something like that. Jean went out and within 10 or 12 laps he was as quick as Martin, and eventually at the end of the test he was about three-tenths quicker than Martin. Jean was ecstatic."

He is massively aggressive inside the car, but the opposite outside it

Donnelly recalls the contradiction of his new team-mate. "Jean was fiery but placid [depending on the circumstances], usually happy-go-lucky. He felt very much part of the team, part of the family. I think there was a lot of EJ's [Eddie Jordan's] influence there, sort of calmed him down. And he was getting results. It's like most things: when it's going well it just flows, when it's as it had been with ORECA it's very difficult. We didn't have a motor home, we only had a truck. One interesting aspect is that he'd sometimes lie down in the truck and have a kip for an hour at a time." Generally drivers don't or *can't* do this.

"Jean was easy," Jordan says. "He is massively aggressive in the car but the opposite outside the car. The way he put himself across was as quite single-minded, good fun, generous by nature — not *lavish* but generous with his time, his mind and his personality. He is also generous in terms of gratitude. I'll give you an example. He'd send a couple of airline tickets to go and visit him in Chamonix — something that you wouldn't even dream about doing. He'd wait until he could hire the best room in his favourite hotel, a little tiny chateau facing right up Mont Blanc.

"It happened in February 1990 — the weekend of the 24-hour ice race which he finished second in [beating among others rally specialists Ari Vatenen and Stig Blomqvist!]. I knew nothing about it beforehand. He arranged for the best guide to take us half way up Mont Blanc. It's the thought that is important because it actually took a lot of organising, but the Alesis are that type of people, strong family, and the family were always behind Jean."

Donnelly approached having Alesi as a team-mate with ambivalence. He didn't really know what to expect. "In 1988 ORECA were also-rans and as far as I was concerned Jean was just another driver. I'd hardly spoken to him. The guy was there, if you like, making up the numbers. At the end of 1988 I was in negotiation with Lotus for the second drive beside Nelson Piquet but he negotiated a contract whereby you weren't allowed to pass him in the race. EJ offered me a good deal for 3000, he was actually paying me and I think EJ threw Jean a lifeline.

Twice he screwed up my quick laps — I didn't know what he was doing

---

"I got on fine with him. His English wasn't that good. You could hold a conversation with him but you had to *wait*. You couldn't rush him. Certainly by the end of 1989 his English was a lot better. We had a lot of fun. He took the mickey out of EJ big time about EJ's rug, his hairpiece, which nobody else in the team dared do. EJ had a soft spot for him and he got away with it. Jean had a good sense of humour. Do you remember at Brands Hatch on the podium when he was wearing a Batman mask . . ?"

Jordan retraces how 1989 unfolded. "Jean made himself into a winner. He started off very shakily with us at Silverstone, the first race." Alesi finished fourth though not before he'd crashed with Bernard. On lap 2, approaching Chapel, the curve before the long straight, Alesi ran onto the grass and returned, nosing Bernard off. "Eric's shunt was very impressive," Alesi said. "Up in the air. When I got back off the grass the car went right and I couldn't avoid him."

Bernard remembers this, their only major crash in all their years of competition. "I was on the front row and I missed my start. He went past, I re-took him, he went off onto the grass and came back across the grass. I was going in a straight line and he T-boned me. I was in a bad state — the car in four pieces. After the race Jean came to see me. He was nearly in tears. He said he hadn't done it on purpose and he was devastated. That proves we had a certain friendship in spite of everything." Danielsson won in 55m 31.92s, Alesi — originally fifth but elevated to fourth when JJ Lehto was disqualified for a rev limiter infringement — was far behind on 55m 56.57s.

"The next race I was terribly angry with him," Jordan says. "I gave him a massive bollocking. We went to Vallelunga and he qualified nowhere. He had this horrible sequence: untimed practice third or fourth, first qualifying ninth or tenth, second qualifying fifteenth or sixteenth." Nor, it must be said, had qualifying passed peaceably either. A Canadian, Stephane Proulx, was quoted as saying "twice he screwed up my quick laps. I know he saw me because I could see him looking in the mirrors. I don't know what the guy is doing. This is qualifying. It stinks, but I have a long memory."

In the race "after about 10 laps he fell off into the sand trap right in front of me, and Donnelly went on to win it. I was destroyed," Jordan says. *Autosport* reported

From 19th on the opening lap, Alesi worked himself into the top 10, catching the Ferte/Artzet battle. With three Frenchmen circulating in such proximity you just knew this couldn't last. Sure enough, having despatched Artzet, Alesi dumped it into the sand coming into the infield.

Jordan called him back to the factory. "I said 'for God's sake what's going on? It's not you and us, it's the team, we are all part of the team. If there is a problem tell me what you need. Whatever it is you can have it.' Next race — Pau — he qualified third and won. He looked stronger in his mind and once he'd won that there was no stopping him. It must have been a mental thing. I think he needed a gee up. He always believed he was good enough but once he'd done it he knew. *Now I know how to win I can do it all the time.*"

Foster agrees. "Really, once he won at Pau his confidence went right up and he was stunning just about everywhere we went after that, exceptionally so." [Well, nearly everywhere.] Bernard had led Pau, Alesi initially hounding him and Donnelly hounding Alesi. By lap 5 Bernard constructed a two second lead. At lap 15 Donnelly clipped a kerb and the car hammered the barrier. A lap later Artzet and Belmondo crashed, blocking the track. Bernard arrived, found himself hemmed on the inside line he'd taken and had to halt. Alesi

Main picture
Pondering, 1989
(Allsport).

Inset *Jordan
team-mates. Alesi
with Martin
Donnelly, vintage
1989* (Camel).

stole round the outside into a little gap in the wreckage and was gone, not to be caught.

Nor, it must be said, was the background at Pau so peaceable. "I wanted to win the races more than anything, yes," Donnelly says. "How can you sustain a relationship with the other driver through that? You just did. The only time I think there was any sort of acrimony was Pau. In those days qualifying drivers were split into two groups, A and B. The two DAMS cars had the front row but in my group I matched the time Jean had set in his group to something like the thousandth of a second. He didn't say anything to me but behind closed doors he had a major go at Trevor and EJ. He said there was no way somebody like me could match his time. I hadn't been to Pau before and he'd been round it like five times in French Formula 3. He thought there was something suspicious going on in the team."

We've returned to the theme of friendship and its strains. Trevor Foster is convinced that "as team-mates they were very, very good because they were friends. There was no falseness there at all, yet they were competitive to each other." And not just in races. Testing is important, arguably vital, and might have added further strain. This is worth exploring in the case of Alesi for the light it sheds in several areas. I propose to call three witnesses.

The first is Eddie Jordan. "It's interesting because when Jean came here, Martin and himself were always quite as quick as each other. Martin had won some races at the end of the previous year and yet Jean was as quick. I think that gave him confidence. Martin — possibly, possibly — was not a better test-driver but he put more effort into the testing. He was very good at shaking the car down so Jean was given a very good car to start off with. He just sat in it and went quick. He didn't have to worry about it. He found out the way we did things and when he found the confidence — winning Pau — he could win a load of them. And he did."

The second witness is Martin Donnelly. "Trevor would organise a test day at Silverstone on, say, a Thursday and, according to Trevor, Jean would ring up on the Tuesday and say 'French TV want me to do an interview' and Trevor would ask 'what about the test?' and Jean would say 'well, just put the same set-up on my car that Martin has got.' And that's what the team did. Was I sorting out the car? I must have been. You don't ask why the other guy isn't there because, after all, the whole team is now concentrated on you and anyway every mile in a racing car is valuable."

The third witness is Trevor Foster. "I have to say in Jean's defence that he was then as he is now, a 100 per center every time he got in the car. He wasn't really interested in testing. I think in the whole season he only tested the car seven times. He was desperate to re-establish himself and the only way he could see to do that was being quickest on every test day, quickest in every qualifying session, quickest in every race. What happened was that we'd be testing and he'd go out in the morning. The car would be pretty close to what he wanted it to be. He'd say 'right, I'll put my new tyres on,' *boomp*, new tyres, *boomp*, top of the time sheet and 'right, that's it, my tyres have gone, there's not much point in continuing.' Often we'd have things in the truck like other dampers to try out but he wasn't that inclined to slog round and round on tyres maybe a second and a half off the pace. Though the car was maybe *better*, as far as he was concerned he wasn't going to be quickest.

He'd explain that he didn't use the clutch as he found it quicker not to

---

"I also remember he was amazingly hard on the gearbox in qualifying, to the point where you could never run a used gear ratio with him. Everything had to be brand new. If it wasn't he'd come in half way through the session and say it was jumping out of gear. He'd have been doing completely clutchless gear changes, up and down. He'd explain that he didn't use the clutch because he found it quicker not to use it — 'in qualifying, to do the gear changes the way I do is worth a tenth or two tenths of a second.' You'd think to yourself *how on earth are we going to finish a race with the gearbox?* I talked to him about it." The conversation went like this . . .

Foster: Jean, what concerns me is that even if we put brand new gears and dog rings in for the race you're not going to finish. The car won't do more than 20 laps.

Alesi: Don't worry, in the race it won't be a problem. Obviously I know that if I do what I do in qualifying I will not finish.

"And, you know," Foster says, "it never was a problem in the races.

I got on with Jean fine. When he first arrived his English was not very good because he hadn't run with an English team before so there were times when he wasn't quite sure what to say. We used to assume that he was quiet or whatever, but really he was fine. He's got this depth to him, this drop of Italian in him — as Eddie used to say — that is *passionate*. He was a bit tearful here and there."

Departing Pau on 15 May, Danielsson had 13 points, Alesi 12, Donnelly 9. The next race, Jerez, was on 4 June. Alesi qualified on the third row but "I made a really bad start and ran wide coming out of the first corner. Emanuele Naspetti went inside and as I came back on line he went over my wheel." Alesi's car had minor damage — and a black tyre mark on the nose cone — and the steering wasn't quite right. Bernard won, Alesi fifth. Alesi 14 points, Danielsson 13, Apicella and Comas 10, Donnelly and Bernard 9. The drivers could contemplate a long break before Pergusa on 23 July. Avignon in summer is a nice place to be and Silverstone's not so bad, either. Donnelly had a testing contract with Lotus and would be doing a bit of that work for them there. Anyway nothing could disturb the tranquil and fallow days to 23 July.

Could it?

• CHAPTER FOUR •

The week
of destiny

ON SATURDAY 1 July 1989, Derek Warwick took part in a celebrity karting hillclimb in Jersey, where he lived. The kart spun backwards and struck a transit van. Warwick felt as if a "sledge-hammer" had hit him and was taken to the island's General Hospital with internal bleeding. The French Grand Prix at Paul Ricard was the following Sunday. He anticipated making a final decision on the Wednesday about whether he'd be fit enough to drive his Arrows there.

Donnelly was going to a friend's wedding in Ireland on the Saturday of the French Grand Prix meeting. He had no reason to go to Paul Ricard. The groom "was one of my personal sponsors. He'd helped me right from Formula Ford days and bought me my first road car to come to England with. Before that I'd had *scrappers*."

Ken Tyrrell confronted a delicate problem. "We had an arrangement with Michele Alboreto (who'd left Ferrari at the end of 1988 and driven five Grands Prix for Tyrrell this season). He could run with Marlboro, who sponsored him, on his overalls until — and if — we obtained another cigarette sponsor. Well, we did obtain a cigarette sponsor, R.J. Reynolds (Camel) from the French Grand Prix onwards. Michele said 'I am not prepared to wear Camel overalls' and we had a dispute about it. We reminded him of what was written in his contract but he didn't want to do it. OK, because he didn't want to do it I had to bring in a reserve driver in case Michele carried out his threat and would not drive in the French Grand Prix. My first thoughts had been for Donnelly but then I heard he had an option to drive for Lotus so there would be no point in driving for me."

Tyrrell was thinking logically. Donnelly had the testing contract and if Alboreto departed permanently Tyrrell would need a driver for the rest of the season. Lotus might be unwilling to release Donnelly or might ask a lot of money for him — Donnelly had just gone exceptionally well in the Silverstone testing. Better, surely, to go for a driver free of any Formula 1 obligations. Trevor Foster believes Lotus were content to release Donnelly but only for this one race, "not more, and Ken wasn't prepared to go along those lines."

Tyrrell looked up to see who was leading the Formula 3000 championship, which is where the stars of tomorrow would come from. "I saw this man called J. Alesi." Tyrrell, who might so easily have been on the Elf jury at Winfield in 1983, had no idea how the name was pronounced even. "You have to remember that half way through the season someone leading the Formula 3000 has to be pretty good to be doing that. And if you can't get the person you know about — and the person I knew about was Donnelly — you're not going to be far wrong in taking the championship leader. You're only talking about a driver for one race and he's only there for that because you're hoping to sort the problem with Alboreto out. It wasn't a long-term thing we were looking at initially."

Sunday 2 July. Alboreto, still resolutely loyal to Marlboro, stood his ground, Warwick lay in hospital, and Eddie Jordan sensed a twin opportunity. If he acted swiftly and deftly enough he might place *both* his drivers in the French Grand Prix. He locked on to the potential Arrows vacancy first. "Rather than go through the team, I rang Derek's wife Rhonda. I've known Derek a long time. I rang Rhonda to see how he was and she said that of course Derek would love to speak to me but 'he's in hospital, here's the number.'" Jordan telephoned Jersey General. The conversation went like this . . .

Jordan: Look, Derek, this is the situation. Are you in a position to drive in France?

Warwick: I don't think so.

Jordan: Derek, rather than doing things behind people's backs, I would like you — and you have my word, so it will all be under your control — to give Donnelly the chance to drive the Arrows car. I would like you to recommend him. If you are not in a position to do this we will stand down gracefully but we would like to substitute for you if you need it. Your seat is not under threat. We need to do our 3000 but it's a free weekend from that and I'd love to see if I can get him a drive. I'll ring you back tomorrow.

That was late Sunday night.

Monday 3 July. Jordan did ring back. The conversation went like this . . .

Warwick: I can't move. I'm under the doctor and it's unlikely I'll be able to drive, but I want your word that if I'm fit enough for Ricard I can drive.

Jordan: I swear.

Almost from nowhere, Alesi would find himself in Formula 1 in a Tyrrell (Allsport).

Warwick: Well, I have rung Jackie Oliver [running Arrows] and I have recommended Donnelly on the basis that we have an agreement about what is happening.

Jordan: Perfect.

Two hours later Jordan "had a ring from Jackie Oliver. I said 'look, here is the situation, we would like to be paid this amount of money.' OK. I signed an agreement with them late Monday."

Donnelly was still planning to fly to the wedding. "Unbeknown to me, Eddie was working away in the background. He came on the phone and said 'right, I've got you a deal with Arrows. You've got to go off to the factory for a seat fitting.'" Donnelly went.

"Then," Jordan says, "I had a call from Moscow . . ."

Duncan Lee was there on business and was a pivotal figure: Camel backed Jordan in 3000 and now Tyrrell in Formula 1. Clearly the attraction of placing Alesi in a Tyrrell for Ricard was potent for all the obvious reasons. So Jordan's phone rang "in the middle of the night. My missus was about to pop because we'd just had a baby and we were getting minimum sleep as it was. The calls went on all night, it was like the Moscow Hot Line, but I was determined to try and get both my drivers in on the same day. Duncan had, I think, been on the phone to Ken about Donnelly." The Lee-Jordan conversation went like this . . .

Lee: Eddie, I need to talk to you about Martin Donnelly. I may be able to get him a drive at the Grand Prix. Do you think he's good enough?

Jordan: First of all I have to say that this afternoon I have agreed terms with Arrows for him to replace Warwick.

Lee: Christ, how have you done that?

Jordan explained.

There remained Tyrrell — and Alesi.

Tuesday 4 July. Almost as Ken Tyrrell was looking up Alesi's record in Formula 3000 his phone rang. It was Fred Rogers, Eddie Jordan's partner. The conversation went like this . . .

Rogers: You ought to try this boy Alesi. He's good. I think you might even find he's quicker than Donnelly.

Tyrrell: Right, bring him over.

"I had a hell of a job with Ken," Jordan says, "because, to Ken's

The men who unwittingly opened up Formula 1 to Donnelly and Alesi: Michele Alboreto (Footwork) *and Derek Warwick* (Camel).

credit, he readily admitted that he had never heard of Alesi, didn't know anything about him." Foster explains that "Tyrrell were very short of money and were keen to entice a bit of extra off Camel. Lotus [who Camel also sponsored] weren't going as well as Camel would have liked and there was a little bit more money to go onto another Formula 1 car. That's really where the presssure came from to make the whole thing happen." The negotiations continued through Tuesday, with Tyrrell giving Alboreto an ultimatum in the afternoon. Alboreto continued to stand his ground. There was a vacancy at Tyrrell.

Wednesday 5 July. "I never told Jean!" Jordan says. "I spoke to his brother. We wouldn't tell Jean in case it fell through. That would have been a big, big disappointment, especially because it was the French Grand Prix. He was put on a plane with his brother to London not knowing fully what was happening. We went to Ken Tyrrell's and Ken's first words were *now remember, son, this is going to be incredibly hard and you must not worry if you don't qualify. The chances of even qualifying are going to be difficult.* At this stage Ken had no money, maybe eight engines in his whole repertoire, no spare car, nothing."

Tyrrell remembers that "Eddie and Fred came to my office with Jean and he looked a likely lad so I signed him up for just the one race." (Donnelly is sure that when Alesi realised what had gone on he "was giving EJ a hard time, a really hard time, even though he was managed by EJ. He was French, it was the French Grand Prix and if anything he should have got first choice. EJ should have got him the Arrows drive, not me.")

Thursday 6 July. Jordan and Alesi "arrived at Paul Ricard in the morning. We knew Jean was in then, that he'd been accepted (Alesi needed a super-licence to compete in F1, which Jordan had been getting). I bet Ken he would outqualify his regular driver Jonathan Palmer."

Alboreto arrived and hoped a compromise could be reached. He'd miss this race and resume at the British a week later. He remained, however, unhappy about the pressure being put on him to change from Marlboro to Camel. "It all happened so quickly," Alesi says. "I

The moment of Jean Alesi's life. He crosses the line to win the Canadian Grand Prix, 1995 (ICN UK Bureau).

This page *A career on the edge and over it: Italy, and a spin following Gerhard Berger 1990; Italy 1991; meeting Michael Schumacher at Monaco, 1992* (Allsport/ Vandystadt).

Right *1992 France* **Inset** *Hungary* (Vandystadt).

The beginning. Father and son in Renault 5, 1983 (J-L Taillade, Automedia).

Full attack, 1983 (DPPI).

Near le pont d'Avignon (Allsport/Vandystadt).

The spiritual home in Sicily (Formula One Pictures).

In Sicily with wife Laurence, a marriage destined not to last, and alone against a timeless backdrop (Formula One Pictures).

Full attack in Formula Renault, 1985 (Gilles Levent, DPPI).

Moving towards the Formula 3000 Championship, Brands Hatch 1989 (Allsport).

Amazing debut in Formula 1 — fourth at Paul Ricard (Allsport).

Electricity at Phoenix in 1990. Alesi leads and locks into a duel with Ayrton Senna (Formula One Pictures).

Left *The chirpy chappie, 1989* (Camel).

Combat at Chamonix, 1990. Alesi (white helmet) is driving the car on the left (Thierry Bovy, DPPI).

Right *Concentration, 1992* (Allsport/Vandystadt).

In the wet, Alesi was always wonderful — and alarming — to behold. This is Barcelona, 1992 (Allsport/Vandystadt).

This page
*Loved ones,
past and
present*
(Formula One
Pictures).

Right *Alesi and
Nigel Mansell
in Japan 1994:
sublime
combat, fierce
but fair*
(Allsport).

Below right
*With Kumiko
Goto, Italy 1995*
(Formula One
Pictures).

The geometry of Barcelona (Allsport/ Vandystadt).

Skittles in France 1995? (Allsport).

Friction? Alesi with Todt, Silverstone, 1995 (Allsport/ Vandystadt).

Imola 1995, a year after the deaths of Senna and Roland Ratzenberger (Allsport).

Crashing out. Alesi's last race for Ferrari ends when he collides with Schumacher at Adelaide (Allsport).

A homecoming. Benetton launches the 1996 car in Sicily. Fans bore a banner saying "Alesi, your hour has come" (LAT).

had not even time for a seat fitting. I was using a padded version of Alboreto's seat and I wasn't comfortable. Ken said he would not judge me on one race."

Friday 7 July. The replacement of Alboreto by Alesi was announced before the untimed session, couched inevitably in the phrases of publicity-speak. Alesi said: "Naturally I am thrilled at the prospect of driving a Grand Prix car, especially for such a famous and experienced team as Tyrrell, even though it is only for one race. It gives me the chance to show what I can do and I am very grateful to Tyrrell, Camel and Eddie Jordan for the opportunity." Ken Tyrrell said: "We are still hoping that Michele Alboreto will be able to resume his driving role with us alongside Jonathan Palmer from Silverstone onwards but for now we look forward to working with the talented Jean Alesi here in France and wish him every success on his first Grand Prix appearance."

It was an important day. Eric Bernard would clamber into a Lola and Bertrand Gachot into an Onyx further down the pit lane for their own debuts; not to mention Donnelly in the Arrows.

Understandably Alesi covered a lot of laps in the untimed session: 30 (Palmer did 21) and finished the session seventh (Palmer fifteenth). Nigel Roebuck wrote in *Autosport*:

Alesi wowed everyone with a truly remarkable performance. Like the Ghost of Christmas Future, he rattled some of the old Scrooges who have been knocking round Formula 1 for too long. He wasn't out of control either. He wasn't a wild youngster. It all seemed to be carefully planned and orchestrated.

Alesi made six runs and here is his rate of progress:

Run	Laps	Best time
1	7	1:13.173
2	8	1:12.352
3	3	1:12.212
4	5	1:11.237
5	3	1:11.547
6	4	1:09.845

Each best time was set at or near the end of the runs, specifically the last laps of runs 1, 2, 3, 5, the second last laps of 4 and 6. He was learning, building, climaxing. Seven drivers finished the session with times of 1:09 — Gerhard Berger and Mansell (Ferrari), Boutsen (Williams), Ivan Capelli (Leyton House), Alesi, Riccardo Patrese (Williams) and Sandro Nannini (Benetton). Alesi had pitched himself into good company already. Still more remarkable was that only Senna and Prost in the Marlboro McLaren Hondas penetrated the 1:08's.

Alesi slipped back in first qualifying, although Palmer's car caught fire and Alesi's had to be shared. Harvey Postlethwaite, the designer, offers a revealing anecdote about Alesi's driving. "We had a bit of flexibility in one of the uprights in the front suspension. It was nothing dangerous but two bolts would sometimes touch as the wheel was going round. The second time Jean drove the car he said 'you know, I can hear something from that corner of the car, a little rubbing noise.' How on earth he could be aware of that I can't imagine."

Saturday 8 July. Alesi was seventeenth in second qualifying, translating to the eighth row of the grid. Jordan had lost his bet. Palmer was on the fifth. (Donnelly incidentally was on the seventh, which did not enrapture regular Arrows driver Eddie Cheever, on the last row.)

"One thing I noticed immediately," Ken Tyrrell says, "was that he had that arrogance which all the great drivers have. It's not a matter of conceit as much as enormous self-belief. He knows he's good."

Sunday 9 July. The start of the race went frantically wrong, Gugelmin (Leyton House) riding up over at least two cars and causing chaos. The race was halted. Donnelly had been helplessly involved in this multiple crash. "I just clipped the back of Capelli (in the other Leyton House), somebody like that, and got a small kink on the front right wishbone. With a few minutes to go to the re-start someone spotted it. The guys tried to change it in the time left and realised it wasn't going to happen so I had to get into the spare car which was set up for Cheever." Donnelly would take the re-start from the pit lane.

This time they moved away cleanly and Alesi completed the opening lap tenth. He took Gachot next lap and ran ninth to lap 15; rose methodically so that by lap 29 he was sixth and in the points. It became fourth as others stopped for tyres and now he contested third place with Capelli. On lap 40 Nannini dropped out (suspension), making Capelli second, Alesi third, and on lap 43 Capelli dropped out (electrics).

Jean Alesi ran second to Prost.

He completed four laps there before the team called him in for tyres. "I felt great in the car, so good in fact that I was not really keen to come in. I was surprised by how quickly the second set went off but otherwise there was no problem with the car." He circled fourth to the end. "The hardest thing was taking time to judge the best places on the circuit to overtake, which is why it took me a few laps to get past my team-mate (on lap 19). It was marvellous to be second at half-distance but really I was concentrating on taking advantage of other people's stops."

Jean was fit — he did a lot of cycling and cross-country skiing

---

Already this season Herbert had scored on his debut, fourth in the Benetton in Brazil. Before that, no driver had done it since Prost in Argentina in 1980; and before that no driver since Georges Follmer in South Africa in 1973. No driver would again until Eddie Irvine finished sixth in Japan in 1993. The rarity is eloquent enough. Moreover it can be contrasted with the other debutants in this French Grand Prix of 1989: Emanuele Pirro (Benetton) ninth at two laps down, Bernard classified eleventh (his engine failed at the end), Donnelly twelfth at three laps down, Gachot thirteenth at four laps down.

The Tyrrell motorhome, tucked round at the back of the paddock, was a happy and surprised place after the race. Ken Tyrrell beamed broadly at one and all. "Something I liked was that he was quick immediately. It didn't take him four or five laps to settle, find out where he was. In that respect he reminded me strongly of Jackie Stewart (thrice World Champion with Tyrrell)." The French media hemmed Alesi and pressed interview after interview from him. He looked slightly bemused at this intensity of attention this fast.

Much later Alesi told me: "Ken reacted very well. Every time I made a mistake he tried to explain to me why it was the wrong thing to do, because all the time it was a big step forward for me. It's never easy to arrive in Formula 1 and do something significant. First I never tried the car before and second I had a lot of pressure. I was sure that it was a big chance and I had to take that chance. Maybe it didn't look difficult but it was." Mischievously, however, that evening at Paul Ricard, Alesi joked: "Now it's a question of having to drop Formula 1 or 3000 and I don't know which . . ."

Ah, the vagaries of chance. Bernard says: "My decision not to join Jordan in Formula 3000 in 1989 is one which today (1995) I profoundly regret. If I had, probably I would have won the championship, I would have begun in Formula 1 with the Camel Tyrrell in France instead of Alesi and probably I'd have had the same result as the one he got at Ricard. It really is the key to our careers — the chance Jean Alesi seized and the chance I didn't seize. Unfortunately I respected my gentleman's agreement with Elf, I honoured my word and maybe there are times in life when you shouldn't honour your word."

Donnelly says: "To be perfectly honest, my fitness at that stage was not up to doing a Grand Prix distance, nowhere near it, even though I'd done a fair bit of Formula 1 testing. It's all right in qualifying because you're only really doing one fast lap. After about 15, 20 laps at Ricard I was starting to suffer. I spun and went straight on at the first corner because I was having a go at Modena. He was on Pirellis and I got held up for a long time behind him. Desperate men do desperate things. Was I shagged out at the end? I was *wrecked*.

"If an ordinary motorist goes to a racing school for the first time and drives a Formula Ford for five laps he'll be surprised how tense he is, how much concentration he needs, how much effort he puts in. It's the stress, the pressure, it's the physical aspect of the heat, the helmet, the overalls, the underwear. Now think about 77 laps in a Grand Prix car for the first time. Only Jean will know how he coped and how he felt."

Foster says: "Jean was fit. He did a lot of cycling and cross-country skiing, and that exercises every muscle in your body. Martin wasn't mega-fit in those days. He relied a lot on his natural ability. I remem-

Left *The podium, Birmingham* (Allsport).

ber Martin at Dijon the year before in 3000, a race which he won. There's a long, long corner coming on to the pit straight and Martin said that in qualifying on new tyres the steering was so heavy with the load going through it that the pain in the shoulders made him shout in the helmet — to overcome the pain."

The next Grand Prix, the British at Silverstone, was the following week and did not clash with the next Formula 3000, at Pergusa on 23 July. "OK, he finished fourth in his first Grand Prix, pretty special, and that was that," Tyrrell says. "I was still hoping to sort out the problem with Michele, trying to get him to change his mind but he wouldn't. I signed up Jean again as a reserve driver on another one-race deal. Michele got all upset."

At Silverstone Alesi qualified on the eleventh row and estimated he gained "six places or so" on the first lap. By one-third distance he was behind Philippe Alliot (Lola). "I had been trying lap after lap to get past him. I tried left, right, left again but he doesn't know how to be passed." Alliot had been in Grand Prix racing since 1984 and this was his seventy second race. Alesi's self-confidence was such that he felt able to criticise him. "There was a lot of turbulence because I was following him so closely and it caught me out. It was a great pity I couldn't re-start because the car was perfectly OK." He'd been seventh and, exiting Copse corner, spun onto the grass then across the track to the infield where he sat gesturing for a push start. He didn't get one. "I made some mistakes after Ricard."

Following Silverstone Tyrrell confirmed that they had signed Alesi for the rest of the season and beyond. "Alboreto wanted to leave so we agreed to tear the contract up. I asked Jean 'would you like to drive for the rest of the season?' and he said 'yes!' We put him on a three-and-a-half year contract." Tyrrell conceded at the time that "if Jean wants to do the remaining Formula 3000 races we will have to find a temporary replacement [for a man who himself had been a temporary replacement only two weeks before]. After all, 1989 is a learning year for him, a chance to adapt to Formula 1 and experience new circuits like Hockenheim, Hungary and Australia."

These were the Grands Prix which didn't clash. Three others did: 27 August, the Belgian with Birmingham; 24 September, the Portuguese with Le Mans; 22 October, the Japanese with Dijon. Herbert would drive the Tyrrell in Belgium and Portugal while Alesi returned for Japan — for reasons which we shall see. Alesi expressed delight that "I'll have a chance to win the Formula 3000 championship."

Before all that he went to Pergusa. The strain on the relationship with Donnelly was showing. "I knew Jean had raced there in Formula 3, at least once anyway, and I'd not seen it," Donnelly says. "If you have raced at a place there are little bits and pieces that you learn, the curves, the lines, stuff like that. Jean could help me with them. I kept asking him 'will you go round in a road car with me and explain them to me?' He'd say 'yeah, yeah, yeah but I just have to do this or that'. It seemed to me he was somewhat reluctant to assist, which could have been a result of the Pau qualifying. But he did it.

Once past Mansell he gave him a 'brake test', saying up yours!

"My first qualifying I think I was on pole. I remember the team showing me an IN board but that lap I was a second quicker than anybody so I kept going because I felt the next lap would be better — and I was like a second and a tenth quicker. I came in and Jean was sitting on the pit wall and he said *do you think you know the circuit now?* I probably said something cheeky like *I think I got held up by traffic on my fastest lap!* Then he went out and was quickest in his session.

"We were miles quicker in race morning warm-up, head and shoulders above the others, and it was as guaranteed as you are ever going to get that we'd have a result. The team orders were: 'OK, you both go off into the distance, we don't care what happens but don't hit each other.' What happened? There had been an oil leak or something at the entrance to the first corner and they'd laid cement dust on it. The lights go green, the red mist appears. I went down his inside, came off the racing line and went onto the cement dust, no grip. I slid sideways across in front of him, nothing I could do: just a racing accident. Jean was out on the spot."

This is the sequence. At the green light Donnelly got onto the power earlier, Alesi hugging the outside. Donnelly was "very conscious of not braking too late because the surface was very slippery but when I turned in the car just went broadside." He'd passed through this first corner, a hard left, but ploughed off immediately after, digging a lot of dust. The car slithered and at the next corner, a hard right, Alesi clipped him, went off and did not return.

"Of course from a guaranteed one-two EJ could see all his prize money going and he was not happy," Donnelly says. Donnelly covered another 33 laps before retiring. "Jean is Sicilian, Pergusa is in Sicily, the family's from Sicily and he had all the family there, the first time in a long time his *grandparents* had showed up for a race. The circuit was full of Sicilians, Alesi banners everywhere — I thought I'd get knee-capped on the way back to the pits!" The championship: Chiesa 15, Alesi 14, Danielsson and Apicella 13. Donnelly had yet to score a point.

A week after that Alesi went to Hockenheim for the German Grand Prix and qualified tenth. He was learning. "I think the balance we found this morning [the Saturday untimed session] on race tyres was very good and I did a 1:47.4 in race trim." That was ninth. "The car felt fine on half tanks and we are looking good for the race itself. For me one of the big problems here is when you arrive at the chicances. All you see is those big red arrows and I am finding it quite a strange problem to keep to the right speed entering and knowing exactly when to turn in."

At half distance in the race, sixth, he spun. "The brake pedal was too long and when I was braking I hit the throttle pedal as well. That meant the engine took me off the circuit. I got stuck in the gravel and had to wait a long time for the marshals with a 4-wheel drive vehicle to get me out." It happened going into the Stadium complex. The Tyrrell slowed, twisted through 180 degrees with smoke burning from the tyres and went off backwards.

Soon enough Alesi would demonstrate the depth of his self-confidence. It's an episode which achieved a certain notoriety and is utterly revealing. During the Friday morning untimed session at the Hungaroring Alesi said this of Nigel Mansell: "He finished a quick lap and he stayed in the middle of the road. He is a champion, a top driver, he has a car for winning races. Why did he do that?" Alesi's blood was up. Once past Mansell he gave him a 'brake test' — suddenly braking hard to force the man behind to brake hard as a way of saying *up yours!* "It was close," Alesi said.

The session completed, Mansell strode over to Ken Tyrrell and suggested that young Monsieur Alesi be instructed in the etiquette and seniority of Formula 1. Tyrrell suggested to Alesi that, for peace and harmony if nothing else, he might apologise to Mansell. Tyrrell will never forget what happened next. Alesi pondered the proposition for a considerable time and said "I don't think I want to do that." And didn't.

In the race he had a bump with Martin Brundle (Brabham) on the opening lap and pitted for new tyres making him last. He slogged to the end, ninth. However passionate he was he had the discipline to do that.

In Formula 3000 at Brands Hatch Alesi led but Donnelly took him. "Jean came across at first but then moved over and gave me room." This was on the rush to Paddock Hill Bend, Donnelly virtually onto the grass by the pit lane wall but having to dart out as he approached a stalled and abandoned car. They passed it with Donnelly fractionally ahead and still on the crucial inside line. Now Blundell moved up to Alesi and claimed Alesi gave him a 'brake test.' Later Blundell murmured that maybe Mansell had a point in Hungary after all. Alesi finished second: 20 points, Chiesa and Comas 15, Donnelly now on 9. Alesi told Foster: "I just knew there was no way I was going to beat Martin at Brands. Of course I tried to stay with him but he just pulled away."

Alesi broadened his reputation round the streets of Birmingham. He took pole.

Donnelly remains insistent. "One thing I will say about Jean is that he's very, very good on street circuits. I knew Birmingham because I'd been leading there the year before. It wasn't an easy circuit because in some corners the car would take off across the bumps. I did a run and I had pole although it was close, a tenth of a second. I thought *beat that if you can, Jean*. I knew I'd been 110%. I said to Trevor Foster *that's it, I cannot go any quicker*. Jean went out and beat me by a full half second and I asked myself *where did he get that from?* Trevor made an adjustment to my car, I went out again and ended up shunting at the first corner! Jean does have an abundance of talent for dragging every last inch out of himself and the car. He's prepared, maybe, to take more risks than certain other people are. That's the only way he knows of driving. Full attack."

Foster remains insistent. "At Birmingham Jean was staggering. Halfords used to paste blue and red advertising signs on the Armco. In qualifying Jean would come back to the pits with both rear tyres blue and red *right round the tyres* but not one mark on the rim. That was total commitment and total judgement. He did a sequence of four or five laps and any of them would have put him on pole by half a second."

Alesi led the race from flag to flag despite sustained pressure from Apicella who couldn't find a way to overtake and tried to force Alesi into error. "All I could do," Apicella said.

Alesi complained of "oversteer in the quick corners but Marco couldn't overtake if I didn't make a mistake. I had to concentrate hard." Foster noticed that during the race Alesi slowed to a safe pace rather than fling the car at the circuit and that allowed Apicella to draw up. The conversation went like this . . .

Sixth place and the Formula 3000 Championship at Le Mans (Camel).

Foster: Jean, you made that really hard for us.

Alesi: It wasn't a problem. I knew he could not overtake me. I've had that sort of pressure from Bernard for years. I know.

Foster also insists that Alesi did not block Apicella. "He never blocks. He just *races*."

Eddie Jordan remains insistent. "Birmingham was proof to me that the guy was absolutely, totally confident and there wasn't even a glimmer of doubt in his mind. To suffer 35 laps in that heat with a car behind you that is marginally quicker and an experienced driver handling it — Apicella — who is in his third year of 3000 and not to make a mistake, that's quite something. I watched Monaco in 1990 and Gerhard Berger was behind Alesi and there was no way Berger was going to pass. If Alesi had been on the front row and made it ahead of Senna, Senna wouldn't have got past either — not because Alesi would have baulked him, but because Senna would not have been able to. Alesi is just that strong."

After Birmingham: Alesi 29, Apicella 19, Chiesa, Comas and Bernard 15, Danielsson and Donnelly 13. They went testing at Le Mans and Alesi did a 1:30.70 before he spun. He departed for Monza and the Italian Grand Prix. Donnelly experimented with several configurations on the car and did 1:29.96, then departed for Monza himself. "Lotus laid on a plane to take me there for the announcement of their Formula 1 team for 1990, which was myself and Derek Warwick."

At Monza in first qualifying Alesi came twenty second, nullified because the Tyrrell was ruled illegal. "It's frustrating, of course, to do a full session only to find your times taken away. It seems our rear wing was the problem: legal at the top, 5mm too far back at the bottom." Next day he qualified on the fifth row and picked up places as others dropped out of the race to finish fifth.

At Spa in 3000 he put the Jordan on the front row, Comas pole, but Comas made a poor start and Alesi led a wet race. Alesi increased and increased the lead but Comas came back at him and on lap 22 tried the inside at La Source. As they approached this hairpin Comas moved tight onto Alesi who visibly hauled the car over to the left, leaving Comas the right — and the inside. Comas steamed into this gap and steamed straight on unable to hold the car for the twist of the chicane. Alesi said he was mindful of the win and didn't want to do anything to jeopardise that, hence the room he'd given Comas. Alesi continued in the lead and did win. Alesi 38, Apicella 23, Comas 21. Donnelly still on 13. Alesi needed three points from the next race, Le Mans, to secure the championship.

Interviewed after Spa, he said: "It's very difficult to explain why my start was good. Sometimes it's good, sometimes it's very bad. I think today for me it was very important to start very well." You can almost hear him rolling the *very* in his French accent.

At Le Mans he demonstrated maturity. He qualified third and ran fourth on the opening lap after a jostle of a start between Comas, van de Poele and Irvine. Prudently Alesi allowed them to fight it out among themselves. On lap 5 Apicella spun off. At that instant Alesi's target became a single point. He allowed Bernard through, giving him so much room there was no possibility of contact. Alesi finished sixth. He'd made his point.

Senna drew up to Alesi — 'I could see it was not going to be easy to get by'

"One of the problems with Le Mans is that the surface is very slippery," he said. "You have to be careful. With no disrespect meant, there were one or two guys up there who have not been regular frontrunners and I was nervous about their consistency. I wasn't going to take a risk." Alesi 39, Comas 30, Apicella 23, Donnelly eighth on 13.

Foster confirms that Alesi handled the race with maturity but points out that Donnelly did too. "To show you how good their relationship was, Martin ran behind Jean although he could have done with overtaking and getting some more points for himself. With about four laps to go Martin wound Eddie up by asking *can I overtake him? I'm much quicker . . .*"

Alesi had no need to go to the final 3000 race, Dijon, which freed him for Japan. At the Spanish Grand Prix he finished fourth; in Japan the gearbox failed; in Australia the electrics failed. You scarcely evaluate a driver's first season, and particularly half a season, in Formula 1 by the points he scores. That said, Alesi had eight, worth ninth place overall and as a matter of comparison (however irrelevant) Prost had five worth joint fifteenth in his first season,

1980. In time Prost would reveal himself as the supreme calculator of a race. In time Alesi would reveal himself as the antithesis. Full attack. Ayrton Senna would discover this when the 1990 season began.

On 11 March 1990 at Phoenix, Arizona, Jean Alesi made a definitive statement about himself and his career. The fact that he was circumspect about it is all the more suggestive. Ken Tyrrell was circumspect about the statement too, but he would be, wouldn't he? He'd seen such things for three decades.

Tyrrell had switched to Pirelli tyres — good rubber, Alesi thought. He qualified on the second row for the United States Grand Prix. Before the race Alesi spoke to Postlethwaite and said he would lead the first lap. Postlethwaite advised that this was unnecessary: the last lap was the one you wanted to be leading. Alesi persisted. He'd pitch for the lead and "see what happened next." As he settled and waited for the green light he concentrated, gauging his chances. He faced a long, broad run to the first corner, a right. Grid:

	Berger
Martini	
	De Cesaris
Alesi	
	Senna
Piquet	

At the green light Berger flicked to mid-track and Martini nestled in behind. Berger flicked on over towards the right leaving a free channel on the left for Alesi. Berger returned, seeming to block Alesi while he positioned himself for the corner. Alesi responded by corkscrewing inside and, the Tyrrell twitching, took the corner . . . in the lead. He accelerated hard, covering the lap in 1:37.346, Berger in 1:39.773. Alesi built on this and created a gap of five seconds at lap 8. Next lap Berger crashed, leaving Senna to stalk Alesi. Senna calculated that Alesi might have to stop for tyres around half distance if the Pirellis went off and, anyway, Senna didn't want to force his McLaren too hard until the fuel load lightened. He drew up to Alesi and "for several laps I followed him closely and I could see it was not going to be easy to get by. His lines were clean and precise and he wasn't making any mistakes." Alesi did not pit for new tyres.

Phoenix, 1990, where he astonishes Grand Prix racing. Qualifying in the wet (Allsport).

Senna made his move on lap 35. Into a right-hander he outbraked Alesi and was through. They travelled onto a short, crisp 'straight' before a left-hander. Alesi stole out from behind Senna and gunned the Tyrrell, grasped the left-hander down the inside and was in front again: audacity *and* reflex *and* car control *and* done to AYRTON SENNA! The instant became instantly famous and remains so.

Senna repeated the out-braking at the right on the next lap and covered the left heavily, thank you. Alesi kept on to the end, 8.685 seconds behind Senna.

Tyrrell "accepted that Senna was going to catch us eventually and it didn't bother me when he took the lead. I'm just delighted with the way we went." Later, Tyrrell told me: "You have to remember that we had made the switch to Pirelli at Phoenix and we were using exactly the same car as we were using in 1989, with little or no changes. It was the car Jean finished fourth at Ricard in. Pirelli certainly had some good rubber at Phoenix but, having said that, in the very first untimed session (the Friday morning) Jean was fastest and at a place he had never seen before. I mean, that was remarkable. Re-taking Senna in the race, that was quite remarkable, too. Senna didn't expect it to happen."

Best move of the season?

"No, no, no." (We'll come to Tyrrell's considered opinion of that.)

"Phoenix was nothing special," Alesi says. "I had a good start, I tried from the beginning to stay maximum on the limit but it was not to be a victory. I understood that we had a car which could be pushed hard so I was sure about the combat with Senna. When he overtook me I braked very, very late but he braked *later* at the corner. He had a problem using the power because he was over-steering a little bit. I had this opportunity to repass so I did it. For me it was another lap in the lead. It was a dream just to race against him. He was my hero. I love racing. I love to drive to the maximum . . ."

(At Phoenix, Tyrrell moved adroitly to dampen the gathering media excitement. "It would be wrong to make a star of him after this first race of the season.")

In Brazil he finished seventh, at Imola sixth. At Monaco he ran

Monaco, and a superb second place (Allsport).

behind Senna and Prost on the opening lap. On the bump-bounce down to Mirabeau — a right-hander and a fraught, narrowing place to try to overtake — Prost shifted over to the left. Alesi stabbed the Tyrrell to the inside and went clean through.

"For me," Tyrrell says, "that was the best move of the season. That was absolutely f-a-n-t-a-s-t-i-c. That was special. It's not the answer to say this was like the good old days. It's very difficult to do it *these* days. That's why it doesn't happen very often. He's got a bit of the devil in him. He's prepared to take a chance like that where most people would have been conservative about such a decision at such a corner. It doesn't seem to bother him at all. One of the remarkable things is that he doesn't care who it is. In this case it was his mentor, Prost. You think *how can he dare to do that to Prost?* But then, remember Hungary and Mansell."

We're still at Mirabeau on lap 1 of the Monaco Grand Prix, however, the action by no means completed. Once Alesi was through, Prost shifted back onto the racing line and Berger couldn't stop in time. They thumped, necessitating a re-start. Alesi ran third behind Senna and Prost until Prost retired after 30 laps, battery. Alesi finished 1.087 seconds from Senna, who slowed in the later stages to protect what he feared may be an engine problem. Senna knew as well as anyone that Alesi would draw up but overtaking was something else again. This was the race Eddie Jordan has already discussed, where Berger pressured Alesi and made no impression.

Here is Alesi verbatim: "At the beginning Prost was quick and I follow him 20 laps but it's difficult because in fast corners you are in some trouble with turbulence and it was really difficult. Slowly, when he had some problems, I take the second place and I push very hard to try and keep my speed but Senna was too quick. I can't finish first (slight smile, wave of the hand). I just liked to stay in second position because it is so fantastic for me, but Gerhard Berger was very, very quick (slight smile again) and I try to keep second place and it was very difficult for me."

By now Alesi was under a different pressure. The publicity threatened to overwhelm him and he was "not happy" about it. Whenever he was in France he spent more time accommodating the media and sponsors than with his family. "That is a part of the life, it is my job but I think it is too much." This pressure would grow. At Monaco,

Germany, and mechanical failure forced Alesi to retire (Allsport).

fuelling it, Alesi's name was being linked with Williams and Ferrari although Alesi wouldn't say what options he might have. In the week after Monaco rumours intensified that Williams wanted him and his buy-out clause with Tyrrell was £1.2 million.

In Canada he qualified on the fourth row and stirred the intensity. It was a wet race. At the green light he hugged the inside line through the opening left-right corners and that made him fourth. He ran there until lap 10 when Berger pitted for tyres: third. A couple of laps later Senna pitted: second. Alesi's stop dropped him back to fifth and he pitted again for a new nose cone after a "brush" with de Cesaris. Thereafter he allowed his aggression full rein and stormed past Donnelly before he came upon de Cesaris again. To overtake de Cesaris he must move off the dry line. As soon as Alesi did that, the Tyrrell shimmied on the wet, snapping left-broadside-right. It howled off sideways across a segment of sodden grass, turned round and squarely rammed Nannini's Benetton — parked against the tyre wall

after an earlier accident. The Tyrrell rode up the stationary Benetton and perched there. "I went up the inside of de Cesaris and his car tapped mine," Alesi said. "I bruised my back but it's nothing serious."

In Mexico he had a persistent electrical misfire and finished seventh. Swiftly, as it seemed, we were back at Paul Ricard for the anniversary of the debut. I sought out Harvey Postlethwaite for a considered view of the year.

"Do you want me to be sycophantic or honest?"

Honest.

"Well, when he first came to the team we were all immediately struck by his ability to go fast, not only in qualifying but also to be consistently fast in the race. It was a great surprise to see a driver so inexperienced in Formula 1 be so — I was going to say be so quick, but really to demonstrate the consistency and the attack that he exhibited at the beginning. That is quite unusual. I think one knew that he had the potential to be very good. What one needed to see, as with all new drivers, was how he matured. It's one thing to be quick, and there have been some wonderfully quick drivers around, but it's another thing to have the maturity, the consistency to win world championships. It is something which only ever comes with time.

"The great champions have all been able, by their intelligence, to bring results when results didn't seem possible. A recent example of that is Prost in Mexico [the last race: Prost was thirteenth on the grid]. Starting way back he drove with amazing intelligence and drew a victory. Now we've had Jean for a year and sometimes he seems to have that ability and at other times not to have it.

"It's rare to see drivers go as well as he has gone as early as he has gone. Therefore he's become the flavour of the month, he's become the person that everyone is watching, he's sought after and talked to by everybody, which has put him under a great deal of extra pressure. It is a pressure which some of the drivers — well-established drivers who are around today — didn't have to suffer. I don't remember Prost being quite so sought after, or Senna, or even Mansell. Jean has had to face this problem extremely early in his career.

"The die will be cast soon, within the next year, as to whether he is going to make it to the very, very top. It's unfortunate in a way because it would be nice if he could mature more slowly. We have seen races this year where undoubtedly his performance has been affected by the pressure he has been put under.

"I'm not saying that's a bad thing, it's inevitable. I do say wait and see whether he has the strength of character to keep himself focused: to drive well in the races and let the rest of it wash over him. The signs are still very positive. Already I can see him learning to do that. Re-taking Senna at Phoenix? For sure it was the spark that ignited all the interest in him. That he is one of the fastest young drivers around goes without saying. The jury is still out on whether he is going to be a great world champion."

At Ricard he rose as high as seventh before the differential failed; at Silverstone he had tyre problems, was as low as nineteenth, finished eighth; and at Silverstone Mansell announced his retirement, creating an opening at Ferrari.

By now something resembling a feeding frenzy surrounded Alesi. "Nobody can force me to drive a car next year which I don't want to drive," he said. Rumours insisted he'd signed letters of intent with

Williams *and* Ferrari, and was seeking clarification in law over the Tyrrell buy-out clause. At Hockenheim Alesi called a press conference to plead for peace. "At the moment I am going through a difficult period in my life. I asked Ken Tyrrell to be here to help you to understand that he gave me the biggest chance of my life. He is continuing to help me now, even regarding my decision for next year, whether I stay with him or not.

Senna is Senna but I am Jean Alesi — do you want me for myself?

"What you must understand is that I am not used to this kind of thing. The main problem I am having at the moment is that perhaps things have gone too well for me. A lot of teams want me but I really want to finish this season first. I was 26 years old a few months ago and I am having big problems concentrating. Nothing has been decided. When I have a decision I will tell you. I hope that will be soon." In the race the engine let go.

After Hockenheim he met Ferrari team manager Cesare Fiorio at the chic Italian holiday resort of Portofino. In Hungary he spun repeatedly in the sessions up to the race ("you have to be close to the limit and for that you have to spin") and tangled with Martini in the race. Ferrari's lawyers met Frank Williams.

The frenzy intensified. Ferrari held a secret test session at their track at Fiorano where Prost, who had re-signed for them, drove and so did someone in a second car wearing a plain white helmet. Before the Italian Grand Prix Alesi said he didn't want to drive for Williams or stay with Tyrrell but to join "another team." It was a chaos of contracts. At Monza, where Alesi ran third for the first four laps — with the Ferraris of Prost and Mansell *behind* him — before he spun, rumours now insisted that Ferrari had signed Nannini from Benetton! A bluff? The hard word was that Ferrari were unwilling to enter protracted and messy legal wrangling to free Alesi from any/all the other contracts he may have signed and the Nannini rumour might force everybody's hand.

At Monza Frank Williams announced that Alesi had signed for him on 2 February, seven months before. "I have seen his contract with Tyrrell and I believe it has a certain type of buy-out clause. Williams entered into a proper contract with him subject to him being able to obtain a proper and legal release from Ken. We told Jean we would wait until he could clarify his position and today we have a tug-of-war between Tyrrell, Williams and Ferrari."

Alesi weighed in. "I signed a basic agreement in February and was promised a contract to sign by Silverstone. At Silverstone Frank barely spoke to me because he was chasing after Senna and Mansell. When I finally pushed him on the subject he told me Hockenheim, definitely. Nothing happened there so that was it as far as I was concerned."

Senna was maybe playing politics with the Williams drive (who knew?) but Trevor Foster insists: "Jean freaked. Williams said to him 'you know how it is, we have to wait for Senna.' But Jean said 'I know Senna is Senna but I am Jean Alesi.'" *Do you want me for myself, not as first reserve?* A few days later Tyrrell announced that Alesi would be joining Ferrari to partner Prost.

The season ebbed. In Portugal he finished eighth; in Spain he made contact with Berger on the first lap; in Japan he crashed heavily in the Friday qualifying. "Just as I was approaching the first corner after my warm-up lap the car went straight on. I changed from sixth to fifth as normal, turned in and nothing happened. It was the biggest accident of my career." The car struck the barrier head-on. Next morning he managed one slow lap. "It is very painful every time I go around a left-hand corner. Like pouring salt on an open wound. It is worse today than yesterday. Just a small movement feels awful. I hoped it would not be too bad in the car but the pain was unbearable even at slow speeds." He recovered by Adelaide and finished eighth despite cramp.

Two weeks later he drove a Ferrari at Fiorano, completed 57 laps and broke the track record. By tradition new Ferrari drivers always do this. It's a form of baptism, acceptance, reassurance and good publicity. By tradition the problems start the day after. They are no ordinary problems.

• CHAPTER FIVE •

Would it never end?

BETWEEN 10 MARCH 1991 and 11 June 1995 Jean Alesi suffered an Eternal Wait. The fact that others had waited longer was meagre consolation. Alesi needed 91 attempts to win a Grand Prix and only Thierry Boutsen, 95, has ever taken more *but* de Cesaris, Warwick, Brundle, Jean-Pierre Jarier, Cheever, Alliot and Martini reached a century without a win. I must add a caveat. None bore the *daily* weight of expectation which Alesi had to carry across four and a half years. None drove for Ferrari, an epi-centre which routinely and sometimes daily sent fermenting Italy into further ferments and routinely and sometimes daily detonated all over those closest to its bosom. No ordinary problems.

When the wait finally did end on 11 June 1995 Alesi wrote (in *Autosport*): "Very often I got fed up with a team which lacked competitiveness or organisation, with a car which was so unreliable. I got fed up with having to 'sell' a message of hope before each race which I found difficult to believe in. I got fed up hearing what some people said about me. That I was too aggressive, bad at finishing a race, bad with my car, bad with the settings.

"Since I arrived at Ferrari, I have never changed my way of driving, my way of working, because I knew that winning was not just up to me but also depended on everything else. I had to wait for all the

elements to be in place. Sometimes I was tired, worn out, demor-
alised, doubting everything after a bad race, but I was always pushed
by a furious rage to come out of this state and push the team. That's
the way I am."

Curiously, of Alesi's five partners at Ferrari, four were compressed
into two seasons: Prost then Gianni Morbidelli, summoned for the
final race of 1991 when the epi-centre detonated all over Prost;
Capelli then Nicola Larini, summoned for the final two races of 1992
when the epi-centre detonated all over Capelli. Then Gerhard
Berger came — and survived. Berger's acumen and ability is amply
confirmed by this alone; Alesi's too.

Here, then, is The Eternal Wait, beginning with Year One.

1991

From the very first day it held an intriguing dimension. Alesi was
known to be fast. Would he, as the saying goes, blow the prudent,
patient, painstaking Prost away? Underestimating Alain Prost was
always unprofitable. Alesi learnt this and other lessons from the
Professor (Prost's sobriquet) fast. Alesi is candid enough to admit the
sheer speed Prost could summon from a Ferrari took him by surprise.
"Everyone thought he was not so quick but he was, absolutely! He
used the car to the maximum. I learnt a great deal, especially the way
to work with my engineers. I saw the way he worked at the briefings.
That was impressive. You think that these great drivers go straight off
and play golf but that is not the way, absolutely!"

Keke Rosberg, former World Champion who partnered Prost at
Marlboro McLaren in 1986 and is a shrewd observer, offers this opinion. "At least Alesi had Prost to calm him down at Ferrari."

Underestimate Prost? We must move briefly back in time to seek
out the context. Steve Nichols went from McLaren to Ferrari at the
beginning of 1990 as the chief designer for the chassis side. "Prost
had just arrived there [to partner Mansell], the car was reasonable
and Prost possessed extremely good developmental skills. Ferrari had
been through a year in 1989 where they'd suffered a huge amount of
reliability problems because they had the new normally-aspirated
V12 engine and the new semi-automatic gearbox. Certainly when
Prost arrived he wasn't particularly happy with the engine and he did
a lot of work with that.

"Although the 1990 car didn't look dramatically different to the 1989 car it was subtly different in many respects and significantly better, significantly faster. Because we felt we were behind McLaren, we had to try and develop things more quickly so we were racing things sooner than we should. We were taking more risks. The attitude I took was *well, we can take a little more risk and occasionally we'll fail, or we can continue always finishing second, third, fourth.*

"Then Mansell went and Alesi came and we were into 1991. I'd never known him before. He'd been at Tyrrell, obviously got some good results there. We were not absolutely sure what to expect. We did know he was very quick from the way he'd been going at Tyrrell. We'd heard some nasty rumours about him being a bit petulant and childish and temperamental and so forth. In fact in 1991, the year I was there with him at Ferrari, none of that ever came out so I can only assume that perhaps he might have been that way at Tyrrell

Ferrari team-mates, 1991. Alesi would respect Alain Prost profoundly (Marlboro).

because — perhaps — he felt he was a bit of a superstar in a small team and therefore able to act like that. When he came to Ferrari he came to a big team and maybe it was a humbling experience because none of that behaviour ever happened."

In defence of Alesi it must be said that Nichols is discussing *rumours*, and Formula 1 is so tight-knit, often so incestuous, that a dozen rumours are circulating at any given moment and many of them are just plain wrong.

"When he arrived he was very quick," Nichols says. "He seemed less experienced on the developmental side, in finding a set-up for the car and that sort of thing. You have to consider that at that stage he was still very much a young driver. He was about what I anticipated in that way. When I say less experienced I mean less than Prost, because Prost was the measuring stick, so less is not meant as a criticism. It's putting it in perspective — Prost was *so* good."

I point out to Nichols that Alesi confesses Prost's speed surprised him. "Everybody's always surprised!" He recounts an anecdote that illustrates what awaited Alesi. It happened at the 1985 Belgian Grand Prix. "I was Niki Lauda's race engineer and he injured his wrist so he couldn't participate in qualifying. I ended up without a driver to run and I walked down to Eau Rouge to watch, because it's daunting and impressive there. I positioned myself where I had a good view but I was out of earshot of any of the loudspeakers [relaying times].

"I remember two drivers. One was Mansell and he'd come through with the car twitching this way and that, his arms a blur, a shower of sparks from under the car — and that was impressive. Then Prost came through on his warm-up lap, smooth, the car as you would expect it to be on the warm-up lap. Then he came through again on what looked like another warm-up lap. I thought he must have had a problem and was still working up to the fast lap. Then he came through a third time still very smooth and after that he didn't come around any more.

"Each time he'd looked neat and tidy but *slow*, no fuss. The car didn't move around at all, he was absolutely clean. I thought *he really must have a problem and he's decided to abort*. I walked back up to the pits to see what the problem was and when I got there of course he was on pole! His quick lap looked exactly like the warm-up lap and the cool-off lap. This was the ability Alesi faced being compared with.

106

The first race for Ferrari, Phoenix, 1991. Alesi was as high as second, but the gearbox failed (Allsport).

"Alesi was a hell of a nice guy, bubbling with enthusiasm. I was sure he did learn from Prost. I think he also gained a great respect for Prost from watching what Prost could do. I don't know for sure, but maybe he had in his mind that Prost might be on the downside of his career and he was up-and-coming, and Prost might not be a problem, and he found out."

Alesi had driven 23 Grands Prix for Tyrrell, not counting Japan in 1990 where he was injured in first qualifying and took no further part. Thus the United States Grand Prix at Phoenix on 10 March 1991 took its place as Race Number 24. The Ferrari for the start of the year, the 642, had been unveiled at Paul Ricard in mid-January. During testing at Paul Ricard Mansell made the Williams go fastest (1m 02.60), then Prost (1m 02.85), then Alesi (1m 03.59).

Before Phoenix Alesi said: "Since I came to Ferrari there has been no problem at all with Alain. He has never had a relationship with a young driver. Normally he is in a team with another experienced man and they both want to be the leader. With me, it is different." Of the immense dimension of public attention in Italy, Alesi added: "If you are not organised to live with it, you are finished." At Phoenix Alesi conjured a stunning lap just before the end of first qualifying to take provisional pole but, trying to translate it to pole proper next day, crashed heavily enough to stop the session. In the race he ran fourth and from laps 53 to 68 second — although no threat to the leader, Senna — before the gearbox failed. In Brazil he qualified on the third row alongside Prost, ran fourth early and finished sixth.

By now external grumble-rumbling reached the epi-centre. At the annual week-long Imola testing the Ferrari supporters — teeming in their thousands into the grandstand opposite the pits — roared that the team had no wins. They bayed abuse at the team's sporting director, Cesare Fiorio, telling him to clear off to the beach to touch up his sun tan and stay there. The venom of it was spiteful as spit. The daily press, wielding real influence, weighed in with Doomsday headlines. One may be regarded as typical:

FERRARI, SILENCE AND ACCUSATIONS

The San Marino Grand Prix, soon after and at Imola of course, became a knife of an event. Prost gave an interview in which he said: "Internal crisis is a normal thing at Ferrari. When the team wins, it is a crisis of optimism." And more in the same strain, with the climactic heresy that what Ferrari really needed was a man like Ron Dennis of McLaren to instil a command structure, discipline and dispassionate procedures. Then in streaming wet weather Prost slithered *on the parade lap* before the race, the Ferrari floating onto a segment of grass and sticking there, motionless. On lap 3 Alesi forced inside Modena (Tyrrell) and put two wheels on the grass in a right-hander. He attempted to turn into the next left-hander but the Ferrari floated onto the gravel. Imola began emptying of the Ferrari faithful.

At Monaco Alesi crashed in first qualifying but put together a solid race, third, although 47 seconds behind the winner, Senna (Prost fifth, a lap down). The epi-centre detonated all over Fiorio who responded with magnificent understatement: "I had noticed a bit of unease around me but I really didn't think much of it." Piero Ferrari, Enzo's son, would manage the team. In Canada first qualifying was wet and Alesi went second quickest but the handling wasn't right on the Saturday. In the race he ran fourth until the engine failed, Prost already gone (gearbox). Someone described the mood in the Ferrari motorhome afterwards as like a "wake."

Race Number 29, Mexico, was undiluted Alesi and diluted Ferrari. He qualified fourth after a fairground of spins and, reportedly, a disagreement with his engineer over the Ferrari's set-up; crashed heavily in the Sunday morning warm-up. At the green light, while the twin columns broke up and fled down the broad, long straight, he tucked in behind the leaders, held station, pitched full right — to the inside — for the first corner, a right. It made him second. Mansell led, Senna squeezing Alesi. A mosaic of movement, sharp and sudden: going down the straight into lap 2 Senna pitched full right and cut back across so close he and Alesi virtually touched. Senna seemed to be forcing Alesi away from him. Senna pitched full left. Alesi nipped out to exploit it, Senna pitched to mid-track to contain

Precision and third place at Monaco (Allsport).

109

High speed in Canada, but the engine failed (Allsport/Vandystadt).

Right *Smiles and champers in Germany — and third place.*
Nigel Mansell won (Allsport/Vandystadt).

it. Senna took the corner. Patrese moved past Alesi on lap 3 and moved past Senna. Alesi advanced towards Senna and on lap 14 had him clean on the inside at the first corner. Senna responded and Alesi spun. Ninth. He reached fourth when the clutch failed.

At Fiorano, Ferrari unveiled the 643, with different aerodynamics. Would it? Could it? At the French Grand Prix at Magny-Cours Prost finished second behind Mansell, Alesi fourth behind Senna. Maybe the car could and would.

Race Number 31 — Silverstone — was undiluted Alesi again. He qualified on the third row alongside Prost but at the start Berger and Patrese collided. Alesi narrowly avoided it. By mid-distance he was third, leaving a trail of disquieted drivers. He overtook Prost who said: "It was pass or crash and I was surprised." Rumours implied that Monsieur Prost intended to have a word or two with Monsieur Alesi. He tried to overtake Berger who said: "Alesi risked a lot and it was quite dangerous the way he did it." He tried to overtake Aguri Suzuki (Lola) who said: "I was about to let him through anyway but he hit me before I had a chance to get out of the way. A stupid way for the race to end, for him and me." Alesi, nose cone thoroughly out of joint, pitted and retired.

Before Hockenheim Prost detonated by launching a pungent attack on the Italian media who had been criticising his driving. At Hockenheim Alesi wore an *Alain Prost le Professeur* tee-shirt under his driving overall, qualified on the third row and led for two laps during the pit stops, finishing third. The overall times suggested a narrowing:

Mansell 1h 19m 29.661
Patrese 1h 19m 43.440
Alesi 1h 19m 47.279

Meanwhile Umberto Agnelli, brother of Gianni Agnelli — who controlled Fiat who owned Ferrari — gave a Press interview. "Senna is the best driver at the moment and as such I'd like him to be at Ferrari. Prost? It's evident that he's a great driver and he's going through a tough period, but he seems less aggressive and with less of

the will-to-win than on other occasions. He gives the impression of no longer having much enthusiasm. Prost and Alesi don't give the best of themselves. In particular Alesi seems conditioned by something not terribly clear for him — perhaps his reference point to the Professor, I don't know." Presumably Agnelli meant that Alesi was overawed by Prost. It detonated, of course.

Ferrari is daunting for a young man with a reputation yet to be fulfilled

The season staggered on and on. In Hungary, Alesi was fifth; at Spa sixth after the first lap but Prost dropped out (engine), lifting him to fifth. He churned round there for 13 laps and when Senna pitted for tyres inherited fourth, becoming second when Berger and Piquet pitted. Mansell led, Alesi two and a half seconds behind and not intending to pit. In a swoop Alesi stole by Mansell into the Bus Stop chicane, Mansell coasting (electrics). Alesi led! Senna, in second place, "knew Alesi was running harder B-compound tyres so I decided to wait. As I pulled up onto his tail coming out of the hairpin I went to change into fourth and I had a major problem with the lever." Senna backed off. Alesi still led! The Eternal Wait wasn't eternal and in half an hour it'd be over. All Alesi needed was to continue to the chequered flag. On lap 31 of the 44 the engine let go . . .

At Monza he spun on lap 2 and was last, dragged himself to twelfth around mid-distance and the engine failed; in Portugal he finished third but 53.554 seconds behind the winner, Patrese; in Spain he was given a stop-go penalty for weaving at the start and directed his anger to finishing. He was fourth. In Japan the engine failed on the first lap.

Ferrari now detonated all over Prost. The overt criticism had been too much. Someone who shall be nameless says Prost made two cardinal mistakes. He told Ferrari the truth about themselves, and did it publicly. Morbidelli replaced him at Adelaide where in wet and murky weather Alesi hit Michael Schumacher's Benetton. "It was impossible. There was just no way to see." That was Race Number 39.

In November Ferrari announced they'd hired Capelli and were retaining Alesi. At least he'd survived.

"I think," Nichols says, "that Ferrari is the most daunting place on earth to go for a young man with a reputation yet to be fulfilled. It *is* a difficult place. It's got such a huge history and such a huge following. It is a big deal, Ferrari, and really it shouldn't be. For foreign engineers it's not so bad because they are more disassociated from it, and they can be more like an engineer should be: dispassionate and logical and making intelligent choices based on reality, on theory and on engineering principles.

"It becomes more difficult for Italian engineers because they are caught up in the mystique and the emotion of the whole thing and they read the newspapers all the time. I was spared most of that because, being a foreigner, I could only read Italian a bit. It's odd. You read about Ferrari *every* day in the papers: full page, half a page, quarter of a page, but always something.

"Then you go from the engineers to the drivers: even more pressure. They are the ones out there at the sharp end. Alesi speaks Italian, he has an Italian background and that could be doubly difficult: a lot of pressure and a lot of emotion. Any driver feels the mystique, the sense of history. Even to me — a fairly calm sort of character, not a hot-blooded Latin temperament by any means — it can't fail to impress itself on you when you arrive there. I think Alesi didn't handle it too badly. Possibly we could have expected him to be a little quicker but on the other hand, because I'd known Prost for years, I wasn't surprised at Prost's speed. While one might have expected Alesi to be a little bit quicker than he was — this young tiger — it was more an indication of how good Prost was. In the early days, certainly, Alesi did a good job and he handled the pressure."

Senna won the championship with 96 points from Mansell's 72, Patrese 53 (Prost fifth, 34, Alesi seventh, 21).

Onward into The Eternal Wait, Year Two. Would it never end?

1992

Niki Lauda returned in the role of consultant, Luca di Montezemolo — who'd been with Ferrari in the 1970s as a kind of co-ordinator — returned as President of Ferrari. In February the new car, the F92A, was unveiled with a "revolutionary technical concept," a flat bottom separate from the bodywork. Could it? Would it? They tested at Estoril and Alesi said: "The car is very sensitive to the alterations we make. Estoril has quite a rough surface but the car behaves excellently and in the two high speed corners it is really spectacular."

In South Africa the car overheated in first qualifying. When that was cured, Alesi put it on the third row, ran fourth but after half-distance the engine blew. Capelli qualified on the fifth row and ran seventh until his engine blew. From this moment Capelli suffered more than Alesi ever did. It destroyed him, in the career sense; he was never the same again as a driver.

In Mexico Alesi put it on the fifth row, Capelli the tenth. Capelli was out of the race immediately when he crashed with Karl Wendlinger (March), Alesi was out when the engine failed. A crisis meeting followed, then extensive testing at Fiat's little track in southern Italy. The objective had assumed the urgency of an imperative. *Make* the F92A work. In Brazil Alesi put it on the third row, Capelli the sixth. Alesi finished fourth after a lively battle with Brundle (Benetton). Brundle claimed Alesi blocked him and it was "like Formula Ford." Alesi ended the race a lap down on the winner, Mansell, Capelli fifth.

In Spain Alesi spun on the Friday, retreated to the spare car and qualified eighth despite an oil leak which caused a fire. On the Saturday, wet, he went quickest in both sessions:

Morning

	Alesi	1:48.241
	Patrese	1:49.756

Afternoon

	Alesi	1:45.903
	Berger	1:46.062

Alesi professed that the car was going well and "we have a chance if it's a wet race." His wish was granted. He created an undiluted Alesi start, anticipating the green light by a margin so acute that you require a frame-by-frame video replay to realise it hadn't been instantaneous with the green light. He twisted the Ferrari into the gap between the twin columns and aimed it straight ahead into momentary clear space but Patrese took some of that and they appeared to brush wheels. Alesi veered away. Mansell led Patrese into the first corner, Alesi out-*nerving* Schumacher to be an improbable third, and this from the fourth row. (Subsequently he defended his start by insisting that his grid position was beneath the pedes-

Getting the feel of the new Ferrari in South Africa, 1992
(Allsport/Vandystadt).

trian bridge and "my rear tyres were starting in the dry.")

The two Williamses drew away from him and he held up a train of cars behind. He accelerated towards Patrese but couldn't sustain it, Schumacher trying to crowd him. A mosaic of movement again. On lap 7 Schumacher went inside at a right-hander and Alesi squeezed but couldn't do more; and now had Senna behind. Senna went by but Alesi held Berger for five laps and then, in a long right, Berger went inside, Alesi turned in — and spun. Alesi didn't blame Berger. "In these conditions you must expect incidents like this. I think he braked too late." The Ferrari travelled backwards, he caught it and swivelled it with such ferocity that he burnished billows of smoke from the rear tyres. "To keep the car on the track when I spun I used the power. It worked but it also destroyed the tyres." He was down to seventh and pitted for new tyres on lap 33, set off again. Full attack.

He lapped — and tapped — Mika Hakkinen (Lotus), who went off the track. The Ferrari bucked but Alesi caught that. He reached

117

Mexico, and the engine failed. Alesi cannot conceal his feelings (Allsport/ Vandystadt).

Right *Monaco, and the gearbox failed* (Allsport/Vandystadt).

Capelli and dealt with him, reached now towards Berger, fourth. In three laps he sliced the gap from 12 seconds to three, the rain falling heavier. Berger gave way, prudently. Alesi reached towards Senna and in two laps sliced that gap by 14 seconds. Senna aquaplaned. Alesi reached towards Schumacher in second place — Schumacher too far away, surely? On the final lap

Schumacher   2:00.724
Alesi   1:51.672

It meant there was only a couple of seconds between them at the end. "I think for Ferrari and for Imola [the following race] it was very important to finish on the podium because all the *tifosi* are following Ferrari and what we did today was very, very important." Was The Eternal Wait nearing its end? "No, I can't say that. The car was quite good in the rain but it is still short of power, still has too much drag. It is not a good car at the moment." That was Race Number 43.

Capelli spun on lap 63 . . .

At Imola in qualifying Alesi and Brundle 'met' once more, Brundle claiming that Alesi put him on the grass. From the fourth row Alesi rose to third before Senna went through and Berger tried too. He and Alesi touched. As Alesi struggled to regain control of the Ferrari it smacked the rear of the McLaren, both cars out and debris strewn everywhere. Alesi: "Going into Tamburello, when I saw in my mirrors that Senna was quicker than me I left him room to overtake on the inside going into Tosa [after Tamburello]. Senna went ahead but Berger attempted to come by as well. I tried to take the corner as wide as possible but on the exit he hit my rear wheel and we spun." Berger: "The incident was a racing accident. It wasn't my fault, it wasn't his. There was a gap and I had to go for it and he was obviously going to fight me. We touched wheels, which was OK, but then he lost control and I hoped to squeeze by. I was out of luck."

Capelli spun on lap 12 . . .

After Imola, grumble-rumblings again. Ferrari were rumoured to be replacing Capelli. *Sorry, you can't speak to him, he's gone on holiday,* people were told. People did speak to Capelli. *Holiday? I'm not on holiday.* Alesi put the Ferrari on the second row at Monaco and was

fifth when the electrics failed, Capelli crashed into the barrier; and crashed again in Canada where — a race of attrition — Alesi hewed a third place as others fell by the wayside. The true context: he was one minute 07.327 seconds behind the winner, Berger, in the McLaren. Alesi confessed he'd driven "like a taxi driver" to be sure of the finish. After Canada he married his long-time fiancée Laurence Bahrfeld, a marriage destined not to last.

In testing at Silverstone something failed on the rear of the Ferrari. He hit the barrier so hard his head struck the steering wheel, breaking his helmet. He recovered in time for the French Grand Prix at Magny-Cours and, after several spins in qualifying, gave an authentic Alesi exhibition of car control and outright daring. Rain stopped the race but the track surface had dried enough to allow slick tyres for the re-start. It rained a second time and a rush for wets developed — except Alesi. "I tried to win the race. When I saw the rain I knew everyone would stop and I tried to go through on slicks and hope that the rain would stop. It can happen."

On the slicks Alesi lapped only a second slower than drivers on wets, the Ferrari nervy, right on the edge. It could not last and it didn't. He spun, a panorama of a spin. He was reaching up to 170 mph when the car broke from him and rotated massively over an escape road backwards, kept on rotating. Postlethwaite, then with Ferrari, insists this was the longest spin that the team's telemetry had ever recorded. Alesi guided the car gently back onto the track and the team ordered him in for wets. "I don't think anyone can say that I lost time staying on slicks. I drove as fast as I could in those conditions." He rejoined fourth but the engine failed. Capelli out, electrics.

He retired at Silverstone when the fire extinguisher exploded (Capelli ninth); finished a lonely fifth at Hockenheim (Capelli out, engine); and John Barnard returned to Ferrari as car designer. That would have a long term benefit but could not alter the team's present plight: Alesi 13 points, Capelli 2. Into August Berger finalised details to replace Capelli the following season. In response perhaps Capelli finished sixth in Hungary (Alesi out after 14 laps, spin). That was Race Number 50.

The fifty-first, at a typically wet-dry-wet Spa, toyed and tantalised. He pitted early (this time) for wets and ran second behind Senna,

Canada, third, and a smile (Allsport/Vandystadt).

who hadn't stopped. Mansell was coming up to him. At the entrance to the Bus Stop chicane Alesi tried to go inside Herbert (Lotus) and they bumped. Herbert retreated to the pits, leaving Alesi and Mansell to contest La Source. They weaved across the track, Mansell probing, Alesi defending. At the entrance to the hairpin — Mansell on the outside — the Ferrari shivered under braking and Alesi's left rear wheel clouted Mansell's right front. The Williams hopped into the air. In the hairpin Alesi spun. He unclipped the steering wheel and walked away. Capelli's engine failed after 25 laps.

At Monza Alesi's engine failed and Capelli spun. At Estoril Alesi spun and Capelli's engine failed. There was a strange, saddened, subdued symmetry to it all. A week later the epi-centre detonated all over Capelli, Nicola Larini replacing him for the last two races. In Japan Alesi finished fifth, Larini twelfth; in Australia Alesi finished fourth, Larini eleventh. That was Race Number 55.

Making a point in Australia — and moving to fourth place
(Allsport/Vandystadt).

Mansell won the championship with 108 points from Patrese's 56, Alesi seventh on 18. It gave a Ferrari total of 21 when Capelli's 3 were added, their lowest since 1980; but . . .

Onward into The Eternal Wait, Year Three. Would it never end?

1993

Initially Berger wondered about Alesi. "I'd heard different opinions about him." Berger decided to find out for himself and discovered that Alesi was a good guy and a fun guy. People are apt to like Berger anyway, and the two of them settled into a partnership without undue strain.

In January Ferrari unveiled their new car, the double-floor gone. Because Barnard had joined the team so late the car was regarded as interim. They tested at Estoril and overall Alesi came ninth, Berger tenth. Berger, candid as ever, spoke of a serious balance problem which they hadn't solved. The car had active suspension and "you never know what it is doing in the middle of the corners." Montezemolo now detonated all over Formula 1 by saying that Ferrari might leave altogether unless rule changes brought the racing cars closer to production cars and thus made the technology of the former more relevant to the latter. In the background Alesi and Berger tested at Imola and Postlethwaite confessed "it didn't go very well." That was mid-February. The first race — South Africa — was on 14 March. There, Alesi qualified on the third row and ran fourth until the hydraulics failed; Berger was sixth but three laps down on the winner, Prost, now with Williams.

In Brazil, on the Friday morning Alesi insisted that the car was undriveable and Berger crashed heavily, caught out by the suspension. In the afternoon qualifying Alesi was obliged to hustle through his laps to hand the car to Berger. Alesi qualified sixth and an encouraging fourth on the Saturday morning but the engine lost power in the afternoon: fifth row of the grid. He nestled into fourth, drifted back to sixth and was given two penalties — of 10 seconds and 20 — for not observing yellow and green safety flags. He finished eighth. "At the moment there is no time to fix all the problems. My job is to drive as hard as I can and stay with the top drivers as much as possible in qualifying and in the races. That is it. I am doing my best in the circumstances. I am driving at about 150 per cent and

Testing in Estoril and new hope for 1993? Alesi in action; looking sombre and just looking (Allsport/ Vandystadt).

San Marino, and the clutch failed (Allsport).

*Pit lane power,
Spain*
(Allsport/
Vandystadt).

Third, Monaco
(Allsport).

doing that means it is not easy to get results. I would prefer to drive sometimes at 80 per cent but, because it is such a difficult car, I have to drive like I am. My last win was in Formula 3000 in 1989. That's a long time . . ."

During a chaotic European Grand Prix at Donington, the weather constantly changing and pit-stops coming in bewildering profusion, Alesi briefly held second place and was sixth when the active suspension failed. Ferrari needed to make a decisive move to harness their resources to get results. They confirmed that they were talking to Jean Todt, boss of Peugeot Talbot Sport and a forceful, no-nonsense organiser. The races which followed Donington restated the need.

At Imola Alesi ran fourth a lap down when the clutch failed. By Spain — seventh, a lap down when the engine failed — Ferrari confirmed that Alesi would be staying with them until the end of 1995. Alesi judged it "the right choice. I was not worried for my future because I was sure to get a good drive but I decided to stay at Ferrari because the future seems to be very strong with all the work going on for next year. And I want to drive the real John Barnard car."

At Monaco Alesi had "a difficult time. My tyres were worn and my water temperature was very high. I had to be very smooth with the engine. The problem was traffic: even cars like the Lotus and the Minardi were better than me on acceleration, but I could catch them by the end of the straight. I was shaking my fist a lot, yes, but really it was to ask for help from the marshals [to signal the slower cars out of the way]. Eventually Gerhard touched me at the Loews hairpin but it was only a little bit. I'd had a good fight with him. After Gerhard pitted for tyres I waited to be told when to come in but after a while there was no point." He was third.

Blessed relief, however typical and temporary: Alesi drove an Alfa Romeo in the French Supertourisme Championship at Pau — as a guest — and led at the first corner from seventh on the grid. He was given a stop-go penalty for jumping the start . . .

Todt would be arriving at Ferrari after he'd steered the Peugeot sportscar effort at Le Mans on 19/20 June. The need deepened. A holed radiator halted Alesi in Canada, an engine failure halted him in France, he found the handling of the car awkward at Silverstone and finished ninth. In Germany he pitted with loose bodywork, pressed on to seventh; in Hungary he collided with Christian Fittipaldi (Minardi). In race morning warm-up at Spa his car suffered a broken rear suspension, which was strengthened but essentially only lasted four laps of the race. "After they modified it, it was too soft and kept bottoming. The car was just too dangerous to drive." This comment provoked a great deal of murmuring from onlookers. If *Alesi* judged the car too dangerous, it must have been.

He approached Monza with some confidence — testing had gone well — and was third in both Friday sessions, second on the Saturday morning and third in the afternoon, translating to the second row of the grid. One contemporary account describes Alesi's laps as "wild and wonderful." That wasn't the story though. The flag came out to signal the end of second qualifying and Alesi toured, waving to the crowd: a shared communion of delight between them and him at being high enough to have a real chance. Berger was still on a flying lap he'd begun before the flag fell. He reached Alesi at vast closing speed. "As I was coming down to the Ascari chicane I saw Gerhard in my mirrors and decided to let him pass on the right. I moved to the left." Berger was already committed to the left. He either had to ram Alesi — "if I had hit Jean I would have flown to Milan" — or swerve into the barrier. He did that and struck it at 203 mph, the car thrashing from the barrier into a tyre wall. Berger emerged shaken.

Alesi made a deep thrust at the green light, running abreast of Damon Hill to the first chicane. Neatly, nimbly he threaded through the chicane, Prost already clear in the lead. On the first lap Alesi struggled to stay with Prost and Schumacher drew up; went by. So did Hill. Alesi's fourth place became third when Schumacher dropped out (engine) and second when Prost dropped out (also engine). He crossed the line 40.012 seconds behind Hill. He hadn't finished second in a Grand Prix since Monaco 1990 with Tyrrell. That was Race Number 12 — this was Race Number 68.

In Portugal he qualified on the third row and, as they reached turn one, Prost, Senna, Hakkinen (McLaren) and Alesi were virtually level, filling the width of the track. Senna, Prost and Hakkinen jostled and bustled for the inside. Alesi sailed majestically round them on the outside. Alesi led! He held that to his pit stop. "I couldn't believe what was happening. Here I was, in first place, in a car capable of keeping Senna's McLaren behind me. After all this

Italy, pondering the second row of the grid (Allsport).

Italy, and Alesi laps Karl Wendlinger (Sauber) on his way to second place (Allsport).

Alesi leads Portugal but would finish fourth (Allsport).

time it was an unreal feeling." He finished fourth, a much more real feeling.

He got nothing in Japan except a heavy crash in first qualifying and a retirement after seven laps (electrics) when he was thirteenth, and experienced the real feeling again in Adelaide, fourth (and a lap down). Prost had the championship with 99 points from Senna's 73, Alesi sixth on 16, Berger eighth on 12. The Italian magazine *Autosprint* voted Alesi "most loved driver" of the season. He'd earned that. In testing at Barcelona in December, Berger, driving a passive Ferrari, was joint quickest with Hill's Williams (both 1m 18.35s), Alesi fifth and also in the 1m 18's but . . .

Onward into The Eternal Wait, Year Four. Would it never end?

1994

The Barnard-designed Ferrari 412T1, with a passive suspension to conform to new regulations, was unveiled in late January. "This is the car to take me to victory," Alesi said. "We'll see at the end of the season but I think we have a pretty good chance." In Barcelona testing, five engines failed . . .

Brazil, first race of the season, proved inconclusive. Alesi qualified third, wrestling the car's understeer, and made an authentic Alesi thrust from the green light to take second place, couldn't resist Schumacher but inherited third when Senna spun off.

Ferrari tested at Mugello and Alesi experimented with a new front wing to eliminate the understeer. Reportedly this worked so well it made the car oversteer. Alesi clipped a kerb and thundered the barrier backwards at 125 mph. "Afterwards I was terrified of being paralysed because I lost the feeling in my left arm." He confessed to being "really scared. I remember the car lifting at the rear and my first and only thought was that there was a lot of space and I could get it back. Then I woke up in an ambulance."

He missed the Pacific Grand Prix in Japan and missed Imola of such timeless sorrow, Roland Ratzenberger and Senna both killed. He returned at Monaco and finished fifth. In *Autosport* he wrote that "the last few laps were hell, unbearable" with pain after the testing accident but, more pertinently and profoundly, he revealed that he'd spent the week before Monaco "morally shattered by the double tragedy" of Imola. "Nobody could have a conversation without these two tragedies on their minds." His mother had questioned whether he wanted to continue but "the passion for racing is still there."

In Spain he was a distant fourth, but for Canada the car had been extensively revised. Alesi made it fly on the Friday, taking provisional pole from Schumacher; and only Schumacher's strength enabled him to wrest pole from Alesi on the Saturday. This was Race Number 75 and astonishingly — in the proper sense of the word — Alesi had never been on the front row before. He ran second behind Schumacher to his pit stop and then third to the end.

The car's handling remained a problem, although he qualified fourth in France and was up to third by mid-distance. At the chicane he went onto the kerbing and spun, came to rest facing the oncoming traffic. He swivelled the car but Rubens Barrichello (Jordan) arrived with nowhere to go and thumped into it, both out. He spun a time or two in qualifying at Silverstone and finished second.

Would it never end?

It might have done at Hockenheim. He held temporary pole posi-

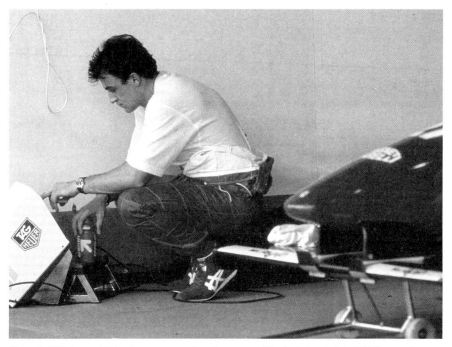

Brazil 1994, and Alesi prepares for the race. He finished third (Allsport).

tion on the Saturday with his first run but on his second the engine cover flew off. "I saw a shadow in the mirror and the team came on the radio to tell me to come slowly to the pits. I was lucky I didn't go off." Moments later Berger went quicker but it still gave the first all-Ferrari front row since Portugal in 1990 (Prost and Mansell). Berger made the better start, Alesi behind —and the electrics failed. He coasted, his race over and not a lap completed. He stood on the pit lane wall willing Berger to hold off Schumacher for victory.

As Berger crossed the line Todt hugged Alesi and Alesi hugged Todt and everyone hugged everyone. Ferrari hadn't won since Spain in 1990. Alesi couldn't conceal his delight. "We have to be very happy now. I have been waiting for years for this day and I feel reborn." And just when you think The Eternal Wait *must* be over any day now, you find yourself at the Hungaroring and the car is "impossible." He qualified thirteenth and was authentic Alesi at the green light, sailing majestically round the outside at turn one and remaining trenchantly there to have the inside for turn two: seventh. He worked up to fourth, fell back to fifth when the gearbox failed after 58 laps.

First qualifying at Spa drew out Alesi's temperament. A wet session dried towards the end, opening up the possibility of a fast lap. Alesi and Brundle grappled. Alesi claimed Brundle blocked him but Brundle pointed out that he needed a fast lap as much as Alesi did. "When somebody doesn't see you," Alesi said, "that's OK, it's quite possible, but after the hairpin I was close to him and he saw me. He has an attitude like a very young driver. Don't forget, if he's in a McLaren it's because nobody is here now [meaning not enough great drivers]. I hope to God we get some more support to the young drivers and put away these kind of drivers." Brundle has no reputation as a blocker.

Alesi qualified fifth and ran second for two laps before the engine failed. He sank to his knees and bowed his head so far that his helmet touched the ground. He described his feelings as "not disappointment or sadness, but disarray, a kind of moral distress."

Third in Canada, where the crowd adored both Alesi and Ferrari (Allsport).

Second at Silverstone (Allsport).

Revelling in the rain, Spa (Allsport).

Would it never end?

At Monza he went quickest on the Friday, quickest again on the Saturday. This was Race Number 81 and — again astonishingly — his first Grand Prix pole. He talked of how much bad luck he'd had for so long and now surely it had turned. "The last time I was on pole was for Eddie Jordan in Formula 3000 in 1989." Alesi made a crisp start, Berger second, but at the chicane Irvine punted Herbert's Lotus. At the re-start Alesi repeated the crispness, Berger second again, Hill third. Crossing the line to complete the lap Alesi led decisively and the lead increased when Berger went straight across the chicane.

Alesi intended to stop twice for fuel and, by the first of them on lap 15, his lead had increased to some 11 seconds. The fuel went in, the wheels were changed and the flickering clock recorded how long it had taken, Alesi stationary for 7.6 seconds: a good, safe stop. The Ferrari's engine yearned and crackled. The car did not move. At 7.8 seconds it had juddered a couple of steps; then it stuttered a little further. He raised his hands from the steering wheel and touched his helmet, an international gesture of despair. The mechanics pushed the car back. A gaggle of hands and heads dipped into the cockpit. People gestured. First gear wouldn't engage and the Ferrari's semi-automatic gearbox would only function from first gear. Alesi levered himself from the cockpit, tugged his gloves off and strode away flinging them back towards the car.

He didn't bother to change from his overalls. He departed the circuit almost immediately, consumed by rage. He took his Alfa 164 and drove like a vengeful Formula 1 driver clean past Linate airport at Milan and straight for Avignon. Jose, in the passenger seat, lasted 30 minutes of this and said *either slow down or I get out*. Alesi beat his own record to Avignon.

In Portugal he qualified fifth and rose to third but on lap 39 came upon the Simtek of David Brabham in a right-hander. Alesi moved to the inside, churning smoke from the brakes when he realised Brabham was coming across him. They touched and went off. Brabham: "Well, I could see Jean was behind me but a little bit behind me so I went into the corner and the next thing I knew he's

Italy, and the first pole position of Alesi's F1 career. The race brought heartbreak (Allsport).

143

hit me. It amazes me really because someone of that calibre really should use the brains a little bit more. It's just crazy." Alesi: "There was plenty of room to pass but he just moved over on me, and what bothers me more is that he never came to say sorry that he hadn't seen me. I had Hakkinen and Barrichello not far behind me but I was sure no-one could have taken my third place away."

In the European Grand Prix at Jerez he qualified sixteenth and slogged to tenth; in Japan, a race stopped and re-started in terrible conditions, he held Mansell (Williams) at bay for long tracts in a duel of attack and defence executed at close quarters and high speed. This was breathtaking and fair; it distilled the essence of motor racing and of Alesi (not forgetting the essence of Mansell, either). "One metre behind my wing — completely mad!" Alesi said, grinning hugely and happy to be third. "For an old man, Nigel was good!"

In Australia Alesi made three pit stops, two of them slow, for a

Qualifying, Portugal (Allsport).

Serious at Suzuka (Allsport).

sixth place which he vehemently felt did not reflect what he'd done in the race. He departed Race Number 85 in high dudgeon. Schumacher had the championship with 92 points from Hill's 91, Berger third on 41, Alesi fifth on 24 but . . .

Onward into The Eternal Wait, Year Five. Would it *never* end . . ?

• CHAPTER SIX •

Alesi at last

THEY MOVED INTO the 1995 pre-season rituals. Early January and Alesi tested a Ferrari with the latest V12 engine at Fiorano. It went well. Early February and the new car was launched — Alesi making all the appropriate noises, no problems with his motivation. Late February and they tested at Paul Ricard, where Berger ran Schumacher close and Alesi said this was the best Ferrari he'd driven.

The first race — in Brazil — suggested, however, that the gap between Ferrari and their immediate rivals, Williams and Benetton, had not narrowed. Alesi and Berger qualified on the third row and the race became a confirmation, both lapped (although Schumacher and Coulthard, first and second, were temporarily disqualified over alleged fuel irregularities, giving the win to Berger and hoisting Alesi to third until their reinstatements).

Formula 1 returned to Argentina after 14 years, and qualifying became further confirmation: Alesi third row, Berger fourth. At the green, the pack engulfed both of them and they nearly touched. "I got a bad start and everyone passed me. I tried to brake late on the inside but it was very slippery and I spun." That caused a multiple crash but not of serious dimensions. Alesi took the spare car to the

Right *Serious testing at the Paul Ricard circuit, 1995* (Allsport).

re-start and settled into fifth. On lap 6 he took Mika Salo (Tyrrell) for fourth but lay 14 seconds from the leading group. Hill and Schumacher pitted within two laps of each other, Coulthard retired (engine) and . . . Alesi led. He kept that until his own stop, emerged behind Hill and stayed there to the end. "I finished second because my car was very good. We improved a lot and I don't want to complain at all about my car because it's the first time I'm driving a car which is so competitive. Williams are very strong, I think we are not far behind them and I am very happy."

Happiness was not a word anyone could use about returning to Imola. Alesi approached it with "strong feelings" and wondered how he'd walk through the gates, how he'd drive the circuit without being overwhelmed by memories of the previous year. He spoke of "these images in our minds." The Tamburello corner where Senna had died, and the Villeneuve curve where Ratzenberger died, had been completely altered which helped in coping with the images. "It's a very nice, safe layout. The modifications have changed certain basic characteristics but Imola has retained its personality and it allows the drivers to express themselves." It must be said that one characteristic of Italian life had not altered. On the Friday evening Alesi and Berger *both* had their road-going Ferraris stolen from their respective hotels . . .

Berger qualified on the front row, Alesi the third. At the green, Alesi made a hesitant start, sixth. He dealt with Hakkinen into the Villeneuve curve but, on a wet track drying, pitted early for slick tyres and set fastest lap. He stabbed and darted trying to deal with Coulthard who resisted firmly and, enraged, Alesi detonated afterwards. "I have fought many battles in Formula 1 and he (Coulthard) is one of the most ignorant drivers I have ever seen. When you start to zig-zag to push your competitor off the road, it is not correct. OK, on the last lap do it, but not at the beginning of the race." This detonation surprised many who'd seen the joust as hard but essentially fair. When Coulthard pitted, Alesi ran to the end second behind Hill — again. That was Race Number 88.

Would it never end . . ?

The disquiet started in Spain where rumours insinuated that Schumacher wanted $20 million to drive in 1996 and Ferrari were the team most likely to pay it. Did this make Alesi vulnerable? Not yet, anyway. He took provisional pole, although Schumacher beat that on the Saturday. In the race he ran second to lap 25 when the engine failed.

He took provisional pole at Monaco after a lap of such audacity and car control it made you want to wince or cheer. Hydraulic pressure hobbled him on the Saturday. At the green, he fashioned a typical start by powering down the inside but, in the jostle and compression of the surge towards Ste Devote, Coulthard moved over. They crashed, Coulthard rammed across into Berger. The Williams lifted sideways and now Alesi and Berger crashed, halting the whole thing. Alesi took the spare car to the restart and, deep into the race, led briefly when Schumacher pitted. After Alesi's own stop ·he was seven seconds behind Schumacher. Alesi fell away but Monaco is a fickle mistress. What if anything befell Schumacher? Alesi came upon Brundle (Ligier) and tracked him. Brundle spun, leaving Alesi with nowhere to go but the barrier. He struck it with enough force to

Brazil, and fifth (Allsport).

A brilliant second place in Argentina. Lift off (Allsport)
and sensitivity in the wet (ICN UK Bureau).

An emotional second place at Imola (Allsport).

momentarily knock himself out and — recovered and back in the pits — was close to tears.

"To block me, he was driving so much on the limit that eventually he touched the barrier at Tabac. I'm very disappointed but I won't give up," he said. Brundle admitted "it was my fault. I was pushing very hard to make up for the penalty I got at the start of the race [a stop-go for 'jumping' the green light]. I caught the bumps wrong coming in to Tabac, lost the back of the car and touched the barrier. I couldn't help but spin. Alesi was just an innocent bystander."

You need the tapestry of Montreal and its Ile Notre Dame circuit to really understand the many layers of what happened there. The city, of course, is in French-speaking Quebec, a province periodically racked by attempts at independence. The circuit is called after Gilles Villeneuve, himself a French-Canadian and still revered. He made the Ferrari bearing 27 a hallowed number and Alesi, a Frenchman, was driving that number 27. These were the layers which would interweave into the tapestry — although qualifying proved strictly ordinary, Schumacher fastest both days, Berger third and Alesi fourth both days.

On the Sunday the track surface itself resembled a tapestry, dry here, wet there but overall drying. At the green, a strictly ordinary race unfolded, Schumacher strongly ahead from Hill and Coulthard, then Berger, then Alesi. Clearly The Wait wouldn't be ending here, if indeed ever. Alesi stole a 'look' at Berger — a gesture almost, flick out, flick back — and the order remained static crossing the line to complete the opening lap. Into lap 2 Coulthard, under pressure from both Ferraris, braked late for a right-hander and the Williams whipped from him, spinning, *as* Alesi overtook Berger. Both Alesi and Berger braked savagely: they had the Williams broadside in front of them. For an instant, the smoke from 12 locked wheels rose like autumn mist. As Coulthard revolved onto the gravel trap Alesi seized the corner, two wheels bounding along the kerb. He set off third.

This was no more than a minor move down the field. Already it seemed all but sure that Schumacher, imperious, would win by a distance. On lap 4 he set fastest lap to establish that tone; and yet, this one weekend the Williams cars were difficult to control. Within

Spain, and the engine failed (Allsport).

153

Main picture *The start of the Canadian Grand Prix, Alesi lost in the pack* (Formula One Pictures).

Inset *Who could know the Eternal Wait was poised to end? Alesi with Jean Todt, running the team, in Canada* (Allsport).

a couple of laps a singular fact became more and more evident. Hill was vulnerable to both Ferraris. Alesi went to the limit, the car visibly straining under what he demanded of it. The gaps to Schumacher, lap 6:

Hill   at 5.562 seconds
Alesi   at 6.782
Berger   at 7.793

Alesi caught Hill but overtaking is notoriously difficult at the Ile Notre Dame and all too often the cars can seem like carriages in a train. The gaps to Schumacher, lap 15:

Hill   at 7.452
Alesi   at 8.594
Berger   at 9.652

On lap 17 Hill had two slower cars hampering him and that allowed Alesi to draw full up. Hill covered the racing line but travelling towards the hairpin — a tight arc — Alesi angled to the inside, *insisted* on the inside and Hill ceded. Alesi was second although at lap 25, over one third distance covered, Schumacher led by 10.215 seconds and a lap later set a new fastest lap, continuing the tone. Schumacher would increase his pace to the point where, in a further 12 laps, he could make his single stop for tyres and fuel without sacrificing the lead.

"In the early laps," Alesi said, "I was thinking maybe I could fight with Schumacher but I soon realised that that was going to be difficult." Schumacher pushed the lead to 13 seconds, but when Alesi pitted on lap 34 and emerged 45.056 seconds adrift, Schumacher could relax. He could certainly have relaxed more if he'd known that Ferrari were deeply concerned about their fuel consumption and relayed that to Alesi.

Schumacher pitted, sat stationary for 12.9 seconds — significantly quicker than Alesi had been — and at lap 38 led by 30.076 seconds, the issue conclusively decided unless Schumacher planned to stop again. He didn't. Worse, Alesi said, "after the stops I lost a lot of time to Schumacher because I knew we were on the limit for fuel and I backed off to save some. Schumacher was out of reach, anyway."

On lap 57, just 12 to run, Alesi arrived at the hairpin alone and

Montage of Montreal (Allsport).

The Ferraris stalking Damon Hill (Formula One Pictures).

resigned himself. This was to be just another race, Number 91, just another run to the end, just another second place. By rote he glimpsed the big television screen at the hairpin and what he saw challenged his credulity.

Schumacher marooned in the pits . . .

Schumacher's steering wheel being removed . . .

"I hardly dared hope." Alesi couldn't know the Benetton had stuck in third gear and Schumacher had nursed it slowly back. Alesi's on-board radio crackled two words from the Ferrari pit.

Schumacher out . . .

Alesi told himself *maybe today is the right one.* He passed the pits and saw the board held over the wall to him: P1. He passed the pits again and saw P1 again. "When I realised it was possible to win I started to cry and I couldn't see the road because whenever I braked the tears were going on my visor. It was very bad at this moment and I was annoyed with myself. I said *calm down or you'll go off. Get back to driving and see what happens.* Montreal is very motivating because

158

certain grandstands are constructed so that they seem to come charging at you from above. In front of your very eyes you have ranks of spectators and you're going towards them at 200kph. Certain drivers don't see anything but the track. I feel I am a part of the spectators. Each time I passed in the lead they rose like a single person. Their 'madness' carried me. I said *this time . . .*"

Schumacher rejoined but seventh and far out of it. Alesi led Rubens Barrichello (Jordan) by half a minute — a lifetime. "I was a little bit frightened towards the end that I might run out of fuel." The Ile Notre Dame resembled Monza, a jungle of Ferrari flags everywhere and emotion travelling like a current in the wake of the car bearing 27. In those final laps Alesi followed a backmarker, Badoer in the Minardi, partly to conserve the fuel and partly to avoid any possibility of a collision. The tears had dried. He was thinking like a disciplined driver.

On that final lap the grandstands at the hairpin *were* Monza. The Ferrari team pressed tight on the pit wall, leaning and craning. Alesi rounded the right-left onto the finishing straight, everything strictly

Done it (ICN UK Bureau).

Main picture Disappearing, Silverstone. Hill — unseen — ahead, Schumacher and David Coulthard behind (Allsport).

Inset Studious, France (Allsport).

200

Germany, and the engine failed (Allsport).

under control. He crossed the line brandishing a gloved hand with the aplomb of a man who had done this many times before. No doubt in his imagination he had.

The Eternal Wait was over.

The whole circuit surrendered. On the slowing down lap, the emotion brought the crowd onto the track and now Alesi surrendered. In front of a grandstand he halted the Ferrari and stood full up in the cockpit waving. The engine stalled. He clambered out and Schumacher gave him a lift, Alesi tapping Schumacher on the helmet. *Home chauffeur and thanks.* Alesi gripped the roll bar with one hand and waved and waved and waved. Out of the hairpin he stood full up again and shook a clenched fist.

And then "I embraced hundreds of people as if they were my grandmother! It was an atmosphere never seen before. So many times in the past people come up to me and told me I was going to win but every time something happened. Honestly there were times when I didn't know what I had done to God." He'd remember the minutes and hours after the race as "a little mad." Everyone wanted to be near him. That night he had a "quiet" meal with his girlfriend Kumiko, Jose and Prost who he wanted to share in the festivities. Prost had, after all, extended the same invitation to Alesi when he'd celebrated winning the World Championship at Estoril in 1993; and it was, after all, Alesi's 31st birthday . . .

Everything might be fundamentally altered. After Canada, Alesi tested at Monza and said he felt he could take the Championship. If only the world was so simple. Rumours insinuated that should Schumacher come to Ferrari in 1996 Alesi wouldn't be prepared to be his team-mate. Perhaps the French Grand Prix didn't help his cause much (he finished fifth); perhaps the British Grand Prix did. From the third row Alesi put together a monumental start, reaching Copse corner as a missile would have done. Alesi exited Copse second to Hill and, interestingly, from then to the initial pit stops

Alesi and girlfriend Kumiko Goto at Hungary (Allsport).

resisted Schumacher comfortably. Towards the end Schumacher and Hill crashed and Alesi ran second behind Herbert (Benetton).

Ferrari now detonated all over Alesi. In the newspaper *La Stampa*, Montezemolo said: "Alesi has made it very clear that Schumacher's presence is not compatible with his. Alesi has done well for us, but I told him to get off his chest whatever is bothering him. It is important not to cry about 'treachery' and not to behave like a little baby." Todt was asked about this and confirmed it was what Montezemolo had said. Todt added "each driver has his own personality. Alesi is up and down. One day the relationship is fantastic, the next it's a bit more difficult."

Alesi judged the German Grand Prix weekend the "worst" of the season — the car broke down — and he rounded on Niki Lauda who, evidently, had uttered uncomplimentary words about him and Berger. In Hungary, the car broke down again and a couple of days later Schumacher signed for Ferrari for 25 million dollars. Benetton announced they'd signed Alesi "for 1996 and 1997." Alesi pointed out that he'd signed before Schumacher went to Ferrari, an echo of the days when Williams wanted Senna, and Alesi wasn't prepared to linger while they made up their minds. *Take me for what I am.*

He led the Belgian Grand Prix for two laps but the suspension failed; and Berger joined Benetton, though they asked Alesi what he thought about it. "I'm content that Gerhard is coming," Alesi said. "We've been friends for three years. To have the reference point a fast team-mate provides is excellent. The important thing is that Gerhard doesn't start playing politics! Flavio Briatore [Benetton team boss] has assured me that he won't permit it. I hope equally that he doesn't bring Niki Lauda because if Lauda comes I go!"

Monza was a farewell, and you never know which way the passion among the Ferrari faithful at the Italian Grand Prix will move — for or against a driver leaving. He risks becoming a pariah and a breaker of the faith, just as the driver coming to Ferrari becomes the new messiah. It did not happen like that. Schumacher arrived at the circuit with a police escort nursing machine guns; Alesi steered a moped among the supporters, Kumiko riding postilion. That was the moment, Alesi says, when she understood the depth of feeling from them to him and him to them. He was near tears. It is not difficult to comprehend why the faithful adored him: they adore a racer, anyway,